PRINCIPLES OF ISLAMIC PSYCHOLOGY

Farid Younos

authorHOUSE®

AuthorHouse™
1663 Liberty Drive
Bloomington, IN 47403
www.authorhouse.com
Phone: 1 (800) 839-8640

Published by AuthorHouse 07/21/2017

ISBN: 978-1-5246-9064-9 (sc)
ISBN: 978-1-5246-9063-2 (e)

Library of Congress Control Number: 2017906950

Print information available on the last page.

This book is printed on acid-free paper.

CONTENTS

DEVELOPMENTAL PSYCHOLOGY

BIO-PSYCHOLOGY

COGNITIVE PSYCHOLOGY

HUMANISM

PSYCHO-DYNAMICS

الَّذِينَ ءَامَنُواْ وَتَطْمَئِنُّ قُلُوبُهُم بِذِكْرِ اللَّهِ أَلاَ بِذِكْرِ اللَّهِ تَطْمَئِنُّ الْقُلُوبُ (٢٨

Those who believe, and whose hearts find satisfaction in the remembrance of God, for without doubt in the remembrance of God do hearts find satisfaction. (Quran, 13:28)

Dedicated to
Professor Chafique Younos and Mrs. Hafiza Younos

بسم الله الرحمن الرحيم

ACKNOWLEDGMENT

This study is the result of ten years of research and understanding of the Qur'an from a psychological point of view and the relation of psychology to the Qur'an.

This research project is dedicated to Professor Emeritus, Chafiq Younos and his wife Mrs. Hafiza Younos. Professor Younos is a well-known Afghan-French pharmacologist and ethno-botanist, who for the first time ever detected the mistakes in the interpretation and translations of the plants in the Qur'an. I am very much indebted for his enormous research in French as well Farsi in the field of science and the Qur'an particularly plants mentioned in the Qur'an.

My sincere gratitude goes to Professor Emeritus, Hanif Sherali who not only edited this work but looked closely from a scientific principles. Professor Sherali has always been a strong support and mentor that I am very much grateful and indebted.

I would like to thank Dr. Razia Iqbal and Dr. Maihan Amiryar for reading and providing feedback and their kind endorsement.

Lastly, I am very grateful to my very young and competent Research Assistant, Nastaran Qassemi, without whose technical support and feed back this work would not be published. Nastaran studies political science and psychology at Diablo Valley College and will move on for a higher education in the field of political science and psychology. I am privileged to have had her in this project. I strongly believe that she will have a very bright future in academia.

I discussed most of these topics on my TV talk shows and I am very thankful to my audience worldwide for their feedback and support.

Last but not least, from the bottom of my heart, I sincerely thank and extend my gratitude to my wife, Fowzia Younos for her continuous support, kindness, and patience.

Farid Younos
Bay Point, California

PRELUDE

Between 2007 and 2012, I was honored by the Department of Human Development and Women Studies at California State University East Bay to teach a series of courses on human development theories and methodology of research. It was a great opportunity for me to realize the fact that my faith, Islam, has touched upon many different psychological principles. Consequently, I have written an essay called, "A Few Principles of Islamic Psychology" in the Farsi language published by Islamic Fiqh. Ten years have passed and I have studied more about the relation between the Quran and Psychology. This field has become of great interest to me because it deals with peace and serenity of mankind. I understand through my studies that without a peace of mind, no one can achieve anything in this life. Faith, *"Iman"*, cannot be seen as we cannot see the mind, is a tool for correcting human behavior if it is applied properly. That means, application of faith in the wrong way could easily disturb the mind and the result is counter effective. The best examples are ISIS and the Taliban who misunderstood their faith resulting in a disaster of societies in human existence all around the world because of the atrocities they have committed worldwide.

This research becomes more important to me as a Muslim living in a liberal, democratic system that we are all responsible for our own actions and deeds. In a system that is based upon individualism, we all are responsible for our good, progress, or failure. Hence Islamic psychology is a tool for better living, individually, socially, psychologically, and the entire interaction we may have as an element of our social system. This is a fundamental Islamic teaching that on a personal level, everybody is responsible to God for themselves only, nobody else. However, proper education is a key to success and the education begins when a child is in the womb of their mother.

In this research, we try to show that faith has a lot to do with the mind, in the process of mind, because religion, as we call it "Deen", is an intellectual property. The true "Deen" cannot be seen, but felt by the human soul and the human mind. Again, like any other domestic animal, the human mind and the human soul need training to achieve felicity.

The purpose of education in Islam is to reach people at large, not a specific group of people such as academia. Therefore, this research is for the layman to understand and realize his own existence in relation to himself, God and society, and consequently be a productive part of society. Using fancy words or academic psychological terms have been avoided for better understanding for everybody. Because Islam is a unified system, verses, the Qur'an relates to different analysis. Hence, there is a repetition of verses as well as of analysis in this study. This repetition is needed to show the inter-relationship of the subject matter.

INTRODUCTION

Before we delve into the definition of psychology in Islam, we have to know the meaning of Islam. The meaning of Islam is both literal and allegorical. The literal meaning of Islam is *Salama*, meaning peace. Allegorically, it means submission to the will of God. These two words, literal and allegorical, are interrelated meaning no one can have peace in their hearts until they submit to His will.

We do not see God, we cannot talk to Him directly, we cannot hear Him, and we cannot touch Him. Just like the definition of psychology says that we cannot see the mind but we can only understand it. So the question comes, when we do not see the mind and do not see God, on what principles do we submit?

According to Islam, God is the core principle of life. He is the Creator, Sustainer, Provider, and Protector of the universe as a whole. Mankind is part of this universal system. Mankind did not create himself; he is the creation of God meaning that mankind is part of the universal system and likewise the universal system is part of mankind. What this tells us is that the Law of Nature and the Law of God are one and the same. In order for us to know, realize, understand, and comprehend the existence of God we have to observe what God has created. Observation with our open eyes is a principle of psychology. When we observe, the whole creation as a unified system; we reach to the conclusion that we have to submit to a Being who created the whole system for us and we are in it as an element, not apart from it. Observing the law of nature is an allegorical principle of understanding Islamic psychology.

Psychology is the study of the mind and behavior. Based on this definition, it is important to note that behavior is also a reflection of the mind. Islamic psychology and the existence of God conclude that the mind that cannot be seen and this is the core principle of all actions known and unknown. Known acts are those that are seen. An example of known acts is seeing somebody raise their hands to harm somebody else. Unknown acts are those that we cannot see and we do not even assume the intention of the act.

According to Islam, that is why *Niya* (intention) is an Islamic psychological fact that all actions of human kind are based upon *Niya*. No one truly knows the intention of others all the time, but people know their own intentions because they know themselves. Islam, as well as western philosophy believes on the same principle. The Greek philosopher Socrates said, "Know thyself". Prophet Muhammad said, "Those who know themselves, know God". This established the ground for Islamic psychology is that people know their own minds, their intentions, and themselves while we cannot read their minds. However, beside themselves, God also knows what is in their hearts. The Qur'an says,

إِنَّ ٱللَّهَ عَلِيمٌ بِذَاتِ ٱلصُّدُورِ

"For God knows well, the secrets of your hearts" (Qur'an, 5:7).

In this case, Islam makes a person responsible for their conscience for whatever they do. At the same time, since God makes them responsible for their actions, they are accountable to God only.

Laleh Bakhtiar on her amazing book, *God's Will Be Done*, established three psychological principles: Theo-ethics, Socio-ethics, and Psycho-ethics. We are trying to focus on those principles as blue prints of Islamic psychology.

The main reason Islamic psychology gets more attention in contemporary lifestyle is because liberal capitalist democracy with its advances through science and technology somehow made humans a production animal rather than a human being that thinks for themselves. Do as the Romans do; ordinary people have become consumers economically and are manipulated politically for the sake of those who have the means of production. In a materialistic society, everything is based upon production and humans are looked upon as producers. This mind set of people, being only producers, cause tremendous social problems such as suicide, homicide, drug addiction, discrimination on the basis of gender, race, and language. Human values are compromised for productions. All this makes us realize that we are not just productive animals, but we are human beings that should be able to think for ourselves. Another trend is, that due to materialistic trends is that mankind has become so selfish that they think about nothing but themselves. All successes and achievements are measured by wealth and production. This is a stage of misery in an industrial society. According to Islam, mankind reaches this stage of misery because they took out God from his heart in the real sense. There are those who claim to be God conscience when truly God does not even exist in their hearts. We know this because of their discriminatory and negative attitudes towards others seeing them as infantile, or that they are not good enough or not fit according to their own understanding of their own religious denomination. These people, Muslim or non-Muslims, who claim to be God conscience and claim to know God, are trapped into religious ethnocentrism that they don't see but their own creed as the only truth.

The problem with not living with a true God conscience mind is that, this attitude will throw mankind out of balance and the cycle of life because the whole system has been created for and a sense of. According to Islam, when mankind takes God out from their hearts, they lose their balance and they fall into different difficulties because their minds are off balance. God brings balance and moderation in people's hearts if they understand the application of their faith according to the Law of Nature. The Qur'an says,

لَقَدْ خَلَقْنَا ٱلْإِنسَٰنَ فِىٓ أَحْسَنِ تَقْوِيمٍ

"We have indeed created man in the best of molds" (Quran 95:4).

"The best of molds" referring to mankind's is body, which is not only beautifully designed but also that their body and spirit are aligned.

In order for us to understand Islamic psychology in depth, we need to know the four basic principles of Islam:

1. Existence of God in Islam.
2. The principle of Islamic research in Islamic psychology.
3. Oneness of God and Creation (Tawhid).
4. Human beings as a representative of God and the inter-relation of faith and psychology.

If we look closely, in the field of monotheism, which emphasizes oneness of the universe and of mankind, we reach to a conclusion that Islam disregards anything in life that is separated or not unified. Lack of unity is not aligned with monotheism. Therefore, Islamic psychological principles are based upon the unity of the universe.

PRINCIPLES OF PSYCHOLOGICAL UNDERSTANDING IN THE QUR'AN

The Qur'an is the book of wisdom. Allah, the Creator, completed His message to humanity saying,

ٱلْيَوْمَ أَكْمَلْتُ لَكُمْ دِينَكُمْ وَأَتْمَمْتُ عَلَيْكُمْ نِعْمَتِى وَرَضِيتُ لَكُمُ ٱلْإِسْلَٰمَ دِينًا

"This day have I perfected your religion for you, completed My favor upon you and have chosen for you Islam as your religion" (Qur'an 5:3).

When the Qur'an alludes that this book is completed, this means that technically nothing is missing in this book and that it is our challenge how to rightfully think, ponder, and figure out these heavenly messages. Religion, (deen), is an intellectual property. One has to completely become certain that this is a matter of mind and intellectualism. In order to understand the flow of messages, as we call it verses in the Qur'an, first and foremost one has to think about the existence of God. In this intellectual process, no one can achieve the desired goal of a better understanding of the universe without understanding and becoming certain about the existence of the Creator. That point leads to certainty and understanding of knowledge in the field of Islamic psychology as an intellectual process of mind becomes much more easier and comprehensive. It is truly an understanding and comprehension without seeing the Creator. So, intellectually, God put humanity into a big challenge of finding Him in their minds and heart. The Qur'an says,

1

الٓمٓ (١) ذَٰلِكَ ٱلْكِتَٰبُ لَا رَيْبَ فِيهِ هُدًى لِّلْمُتَّقِينَ (٢) ٱلَّذِينَ يُؤْمِنُونَ بِٱلْغَيْبِ وَيُقِيمُونَ ٱلصَّلَوٰةَ وَمِمَّا رَزَقْنَٰهُمْ يُنفِقُونَ (٣) وَٱلَّذِينَ يُؤْمِنُونَ بِمَآ أُنزِلَ إِلَيْكَ وَمَآ أُنزِلَ مِن قَبْلِكَ وَبِٱلْآخِرَةِ هُمْ يُوقِنُونَ (٤) أُوْلَٰٓئِكَ عَلَىٰ هُدًى مِّن رَّبِّهِمْ وَأُوْلَٰٓئِكَ هُمُ ٱلْمُفْلِحُونَ (٥

"This is the Book: In it is guidance sure, without doubt to those who fear God: Who believe in the unseen or and stay steadfast in prayer and spend out of what we have provided for them: and who believe in the Revelation sent to you (Muhammad) and sent before your time, and in their hearts have they assurance of the Hereafter: they are in true guidance from their Lord and it is those who will have prosper" (Quran, 2:1-5).

The principle of knowledge by all means is certainty. The Qur'an says,

كَلَّا سَوْفَ تَعْلَمُونَ (٣) ثُمَّ كَلَّا سَوْفَ تَعْلَمُونَ (٤) كَلَّا لَوْ تَعْلَمُونَ عِلْمَ ٱلْيَقِينِ

"But nay, you soon shall know the (reality): again you soon shall know! Nay were you to know of certainty of mind (you should be aware "(Qur'an 102:3-5).

So here, the Qur'an speaks with certainty of knowledge that you cannot prosper without certainty of knowledge and the certainty relies on understanding the Creator who possesses all things and has power over everything. After certainty of knowledge, another step is observation in which one has to observe in order to understand a concept or phenomenon. From a research point of view, observation leads us to understanding the reality. The Qur'an refers to certainty of knowledge as *yaqin*. Yusuf Ali, (Notes 6259 Sura of Takâthur), writes in the interpretation of *yaqin* that the certainties of knowledge are three kinds. "The first is certainty of mind or inference mentioned here; we hear from someone, or we inferred from something we know, this refers to our own state of mind. If we instruct our minds in this way, we should value the deeper things of life better, and not waste all our time and in ephemeral things. But if we do not show our reason faculties now, we shall yet see with our own eyes the penalty of our sins. It will be of certainty of sight. We shall see Hell" In the following verse,

ثُمَّ لَتُسْتَلُنَّ يَوْمَئِذٍ عَنِ ٱلنَّعِيمِ

"Then, shall you be questioned that day about
the joy you indulged in" (Quran 102:8).

Yusuf Ali continued saying, "But the absolute certainty of the short truth
but verily it is truth of a short certainty. He is quoting the Qur'an from
chapter 69 saying,

وَإِنَّهُۥ لَحَقُّ ٱلْيَقِينِ

"Lo! It is absolute truth" (Qur'an 69:51).

We read again the interpretation of Abdullah Yusuf Ali "All truth is in
itself certain, but as received by men, and understood with reference
to men psychology, certainty may have certain degrees. There is the
probability or certainty resulting of the application of man's power of
judgment and his appeasement of evidence. This is *ilm-ul-yaqin*, certainty
by reasoning or inference. Then there is a certainty of seeing some with
our own eyes. "Seeing is believing". This is *ain-ul-yaqin* certainty by
personal inspection. Then there is absolute truth by no possibility of
judgment, error of the eye, (which stands for any instrument of sense
of perception, any ancillary aids such as microscopes), and this is the
absolute truth is *haqq-ul-yaqin*".

According to Islam, mankind has been created with good nature (fitra).
They are made responsible for all their actions, deed, and creed. The
Qur'an says,

فَأَقِمْ وَجْهَكَ لِلدِّينِ حَنِيفًا فِطْرَتَ ٱللَّهِ ٱلَّتِى فَطَرَ ٱلنَّاسَ عَلَيْهَا لَا تَبْدِيلَ
لِخَلْقِ ٱللَّهِ ذَٰلِكَ ٱلدِّينُ ٱلْقَيِّمُ وَلَٰكِنَّ أَكْثَرَ ٱلنَّاسِ لَا يَعْلَمُونَ

"This is the natural disposition given you by God upon which He
originated all mankind. No change (let there be in the work (wrought)

by God. That is the Standard Deen but most among mankind understand not" (Qur'an (30:30).

The Prophet Muhammad said that God created mankind with good nature (Islam—submission to the will of Allah), it is family, society, and others who can be a factor turning people against their nature. The Qur'an made people responsible for their own actions by saying,

كُلُّ آمْرِئٍ بِما كَسَبَ رَهِينٌ

"Every person is himself in pledge of what he has earned in life" (Qur'an 52:21).

Also, the Qur'an says,

أَلاَّ تَزِرُ وَازِرَةٌ وِزْرَ أُخْرَىٰ (٣٨) وَأَن لَّيْسَ لِلْإِنسَٰنِ إِلَّا مَا سَعَىٰ

"That no laden soul shall carry the load of another; and that there is nothing that shall abide for a person except for which he strives" (Qur'an 53:38-39).

Also,

إِنَّ ٱللَّهَ لَا يَظْلِمُ ٱلنَّاسَ شَيْئًا وَلَٰكِنَّ ٱلنَّاسَ أَنفُسَهُمْ يَظْلِمُونَ

"Indeed, God does not wrong people in anything but rather it is people who wrong themselves" (Qur'an 10:44).

As an intellectual being, mankind is responsible to find the truth for themselves. The truth can be taught, but cannot be absorbed until one strives for understanding it. As a matter of fact one definition of Taqwa (piety) is the heartfelt responsibility that leads mankind to research, understanding and assessment about the truth to reach the final truth. From the dawn of history, Prophets such as Abraham, Moses, Jesus, and Muhammad propagated the truth, but they were rejected in the beginning by society. Psychologically, either the people of that time were not ready to accept the truth or because of their own self-interest, they rejected the truth. For whatever reason, God made people responsible for their own understanding of the truth. Through Prophets, God taught mankind saying,

وَعَلَّمَ ءَادَمَ ٱلْأَسْمَآءَ كُلَّهَا ثُمَّ عَرَضَهُمْ عَلَى ٱلْمَلَٰٓئِكَةِ فَقَالَ أَنۢبِـُٔونِى بِأَسْمَآءِ هَٰٓؤُلَآءِ إِن كُنتُمْ صَٰدِقِين

"And He taught Adam the nature of all things; then He placed them before the angels, and said "Tell me the nature of these if you are right; they said: "Glory to Thee: of knowledge we have none, save what thou hast taught us: and truth it is Thou who are perfect in knowledge and wisdom" (Qur'an 2:31).

This is because God wanted mankind to gain knowledge of this universe, to be His representative on this earth, and to carry on His mission on Earth, which is to spread to the truth about Him; otherwise, mankind would not know this by himself. It is in fact, the mercy of God that He taught him. God says in the Qur'an,

ٱلَّذِى عَلَّمَ بِٱلْقَلَمِ (٤) عَلَّمَ ٱلْإِنسَٰنَ مَا لَمْ يَعْلَمْ

"He who taught the use of the pen; taught man that which he knew not" (Qur'an 96:4-5).

UNDERSTANDING THE PSYCHOLOGICAL CONCEPTS IN ISLAM

Islam, as a belief system is an intellectual property. As a matter of fact, all psychological concepts are formed, shaped, and motivated within the heart and mind of a person that has Islamic intellectuality. This means that by all means, everything we do and act upon, depends upon our intentions that are formulated within our mind and heart. The Prophet of Islam said, "Verily actions are by intentions, and for every person is what he intended".

The first principle of psychological understanding is the intention of an individual. The only being, according to Islam, that knows someone's heart is Allah, others don't know the intentions of others, because others can easily role-play. For example, a rapist has the intention to rape but he doesn't attack immediately, for a majority of time. He paves the road and provides the circumstances and condition to rape someone. Manipulations, extra kindness, overwhelming feedback, constant support and help, convince some people that he is the right person, but actually he has paved the road for his intentions. This matter of the heart and mind is extremely important in Islamic psychology because God only rewards people of what is in their hearts, and He does not see their appearance on Judgment Day. This is what the Prophet Muhammad said about this issue, "Allah does not look at your figures, nor at your attire but He looks at your hearts (and deeds)". (Reported Sahih Muslim). This Hadith is extremely important in theo-ethics, socio-ethics, and psycho-ethics because it determines his relationship to all sides whether he is a hypocrite or an honest person. Allah says in the Qur'an,

قُل إِن تُخْفُواْ مَا فِى صُدُورِكُمْ أَوْ تُبْدُوهُ يَعْلَمْهُ ٱللَّهُ وَيَعْلَمُ مَا فِى ٱلسَّمَٰوَٰتِ وَمَا فِى ٱلْأَرْضِ وَٱللَّهُ عَلَىٰ كُلِّ شَىْءٍ قَدِيرٌ

"Whether you hide what is in your hearts or reveal it, Allah knows it all. He knows what is in the heavens, and what is on earth". (Qur'an 3:29).

The second principle is submission. Psychologically, submission means that one not only accepts Allah as the Creator and submits to Him, but also accepts that they are part of the universal system and the law of Allah and the law of nature are one and the same. Based upon Tawhid, when one submits to the will of Allah, they also accept His laws, His guidance, and His will. This mentality and mindset gives them a sense of security and certainty of life. This is why the Qur'an says,

يَٰٓأَيُّهَا ٱلَّذِينَ ءَامَنُواْ ٱدْخُلُواْ فِى ٱلسِّلْمِ كَآفَّةً وَلَا تَتَّبِعُواْ خُطُوَٰتِ ٱلشَّيْطَٰنِ إِنَّهُ لَكُمْ عَدُوٌّ مُّبِينٌ

"O you who believe! Enter into Islam whole heartedly and follow not the footsteps of the evil one for he is to you a avowed enemy" (Qur'an 2:208).

Looking at the above verse, Satan is the antithesis of true submission. If one submits truly to his Creator, and accepts Him as his Ruler, Lawgiver, Sustainer, and Protector, Satan will not have any role in any life. God gave us intelligence and it is we, psychologically speaking, whom invites Satan into our minds.

The third principle is gratefulness to Allah. Gratefulness is a psychological concept that comforts the heart, makes the person begin appreciating what they have, thus giving them a positive approach towards life, and makes them more hopeful for a better living. As a matter of fact, gratefulness, psychologically, is the core principle of faith. Starting with one self, looking at the way we are created. The way we are created Allah says in the Qur'an,

لَقَدْ خَلَقْنَا ٱلْإِنسَٰنَ فِىٓ أَحْسَنِ تَقْوِيمٍ

"We have indeed created man in the best of molds" (Qur'an 95:4).

This verse tells us that mankind has been created with good nature, constitution, and symmetry. And He gives us the entire body to perceive not only His creation, but also to perceive His power and His kindness to mankind. But unfortunately mankind is not only grateful but he abuses himself and takes things for granted. The Qur'an says,

إِنَّ ٱلْإِنسَٰنَ لِرَبِّهِۦ لَكَنُودٌ

"Most surely man is ungrateful to his Lord" (Qur'an 100:6).

Psychologically speaking, this ingratitude of people always gives us a negative energy resulting in a variety of personal and social malaise. Also, ungratefulness could be hatred to oneself, because it could result in depression. Psychologists today indicate that some of the symptoms for self-loathing are discouragement from others.

PRAYER AND SUPPLICATIONS:

Prayer and supplications are a connection to the source of light, knowledge, wisdom, and certainty. Psychologically, our mind will connect to the Creator and since we believe in Him for nourishing and cherishing us as His Creation, that which grants us peace of mind and relaxes us physically. There is a purpose in praying; the purpose is to achieve goodness. If one prays and the intention doesn't achieve the higher goal of felicity, morality, and ethical values, it means they have not prayed. This is why the Qur'an says,

اتْلُ مَا أُوحِيَ إِلَيْكَ مِنَ ٱلْكِتَٰبِ وَأَقِمِ ٱلصَّلَوٰةَ إِنَّ ٱلصَّلَوٰةَ تَنْهَىٰ عَنِ ٱلْفَحْشَاءِ وَٱلْمُنْكَرِ وَلَذِكْرُ ٱللَّهِ أَكْبَرُ وَٱللَّهُ يَعْلَمُ مَا تَصْنَعُونَ

"Recite what is sent of the Book by inspiration to thee, and establish regular Prayer: for Prayer restrains from shameful and unjust deeds; and remembrance of Allah is the greatest (thing in life) without doubt. And Allah knows the (deeds) that ye do" (Qur'an 29:45).

Prayer, according to Islamic vision, is to purify the heart and mind and to make someone constantly connect to their Creator, Who sees them while they cannot see Him. Those who forget the purpose of prayers, and/or perform prayers and do wrong things, means that they have not prayed. Someone came to the Prophet Muhammad and asked, that if someone is prays five times, pays charity dues, fasts the whole month of Ramadan, but he is uttering bad words to his neighbors, what do you say about this?" The Prophet replied, "He is going to hell" (Sahih Bukhari).

There are many medical and university studies linking the relationship between prayer and health. The benefits for those who pray regularly on a daily basis cope better with stress, they experience greater well-being because they have more hope, they are more optimistic, experience less depression, and their anxiety is low. Prayer is not only a medical factor for us, but also a socially and psychological one.[1] Dr. Herbert Benson, a cardiovascular specialist at *Harvard Medical School* discovered "the relaxation response" due to praying. The body's metabolism decreases, the heart rate slows, blood pressure lowers, and our breath becomes calmer and more regular. [2]

Another principle is trust towards Allah. One who absorbs, in his conscious, wholeheartedly the concept and phenomenon of the Creator and he's truly convinced that He is the One Who is the Provider and Protector, then it becomes a matter of trust between the individual and his Creator. Trust is not only the recognition of Allah, but also understanding His role for shaping human destiny based upon human intention and submission. The Qur'an says,

قُل لَّن يُصِيبَنَآ إِلَّا مَا كَتَبَ ٱللَّهُ لَنَا هُوَ مَوۡلَىٰنَا ۚ وَعَلَى ٱللَّهِ فَلۡيَتَوَكَّلِ ٱلۡمُؤۡمِنُونَ

"Say: "Nothing will happen to us except what Allah has decreed for us: He is our protector": and on Allah let the believers put their trust" (Qur'an 9:51).

Allah cares about those who trust Him;

فَإِن تَوَلَّوۡاْ فَقُلۡ حَسۡبِيَ ٱللَّهُ لَآ إِلَٰهَ إِلَّا هُوَ ۖ عَلَيۡهِ تَوَكَّلۡتُ ۖ وَهُوَ رَبُّ ٱلۡعَرۡشِ ٱلۡعَظِيمِ

"But if they turn away, say: God sufficeth me. There is no god but He. On Him is my trust. He is the Lord of the Throne (Of Glory) Supreme" (Qur'an 9:129).

Trust bonds an individual's soul to his Creator and gives him a sense of security. Consequently, he does not need to be worried or be hopeless because he trusted the One who makes thing happen. Trust in Allah, does not mean that one should not do his assigned duties or take proper action and still expect proper and positive outcomes. The Prophet Muhammad said, "Tie up your camel, and then put your trust in Allah" (Bukhari and Muslims). This means that we need to do what is required of us to do and then trust Allah for the outcome.

Another psychological concept in Islam is hope. Hope is seriously oriented, although the substance of hope, trust, submission and anything that connects to the Creator is the same. However, if one loses hope, that simply means that there is no one to trust, no being to rely upon, and no source of protection or provision. According to the Islamic viewpoint, if one loses hope in Allah, he becomes a *mushrik (polytheist),* which is not knowing or acknowledging the existence of God Almighty. In Islamic studies, hope and trust are almost similar to each other. However, as it is common, when one hopes, one has some expectations. When one puts their trust in Allah, there is a sense of security. It is also important to note that Allah will not answer illegal, immoral, and unethical hopes and everything that we hope for should be morally fit and has to be justified with the pleasure of Allah. It is in that format that He answers all prayers. The Qur'an says,"

وَقَالَ رَبُّكُمُ ٱدْعُونِىٓ أَسْتَجِبْ لَكُمْ إِنَّ ٱلَّذِينَ يَسْتَكْبِرُونَ عَنْ عِبَادَتِى سَيَدْخُلُونَ جَهَنَّمَ دَاخِرِينَ

And your Lord says, 'Call on me; I will respond to you. Indeed, those who disdain My worship will enter Hell (rendered) contemptible" (Qur'an 40:60).

FEAR:

An extensive and irrational fear is called phobia. This emotional conditioning is naturally within an individual without the actual existence of a real physical danger. These phobias could be the fear of height, water, animals, tight spaces, insects, and much more. Natural emotional fears have a lot to do with a person's upbringing, atmosphere, political situations, and circumstances, as well as economic situations. According to Islamic psychology, there are two types of fears, one is natural fear, as we mentioned such as the fear of height or tight spaces, and others are unnatural fears, which are the consequences of our own actions and as a result, we cause fear for ourselves. An example is stealing, because when you steal, you will constantly be worried if you're going to get caught. This unnatural fear is the result of your actions. People are responsible for their own actions. The Qur'an states,

وَكُلَّ إِنسَٰنٍ أَلْزَمْنَٰهُ طَٰٓئِرَهُۥ فِى عُنُقِهِۦ وَنُخْرِجُ لَهُۥ يَوْمَ ٱلْقِيَٰمَةِ كِتَٰبًا يَلْقَىٰهُ مَنشُورًا

"And (for) every person We have imposed his fate upon his neck, and We will produce for him on the Day of Resurrection a record which he will encounter spread open" (Qur'an 17:13).

Also on the same chapter, the Qur'an says,

مَّنِ ٱهْتَدَىٰ فَإِنَّمَا يَهْتَدِى لِنَفْسِهِۦ وَمَن ضَلَّ فَإِنَّمَا يَضِلُّ عَلَيْهَا وَلَا تَزِرُ وَازِرَةٌ وِزْرَ أُخْرَىٰ وَمَا كُنَّا مُعَذِّبِينَ حَتَّىٰ نَبْعَثَ رَسُولًا

"Whoever goes right, then he goes right only for the benefit of himself. And whoever goes astray, then he goes astray to his own loss. No one laden with burdens can bear another's burden…" (Qur'an 17:15).

Muslims are asked by Allah to not fear of anything unnatural but commit total obedience to come under His protection. When people are truly committed to what they believe in, and are God conscious, they have nothing to fear from. Unnatural fear, as we said, is the result of our own negative approach to life, our own laziness, lack of commitment, lack of goals and objectives. So when ones belief system is weak, they have to bear the consequences of their own fear that they have created for themselves. The following verses from the Qur'an are relating to fear.

إِنَّمَا ذَٰلِكُمُ ٱلشَّيْطَٰنُ يُخَوِّفُ أَوْلِيَآءَهُۥ فَلَا تَخَافُوهُمْ وَخَافُونِ إِن كُنتُم مُّؤْمِنِينَ

"It is only the devil who would make (men) fear his partisans. Fear them not; mind Me, if you are true believers" (Qur'an 3:175).

ذَٰلِكَ أَدْنَىٰٓ أَن يَأْتُوا۟ بِٱلشَّهَٰدَةِ عَلَىٰ وَجْهِهَآ أَوْ يَخَافُوٓا۟ أَن تُرَدَّ أَيْمَٰنٌۢ بَعْدَ أَيْمَٰنِهِمْ وَٱتَّقُوا۟ ٱللَّهَ وَٱسْمَعُوا۟ وَٱللَّهُ لَا يَهْدِى ٱلْقَوْمَ ٱلْفَٰسِقِينَ

"So, it is likelier that they will bear testimony in proper form (Literally: come up with the testimony as its "proper" face) or fear that after their (other) oaths may be turned back to. And be pious to

Allah and give ear (obediently): and Allah does not guide the immoral people" (Qur'an 5:108).

The antithesis of unnatural fear is trust. Those who submit in trust to his Creator, they have no reason to fear if they are doing the right thing in life. As the Qur'an says,

إِنَّ ٱلَّذِينَ هُم مِّنْ خَشْيَةِ رَبِّهِم مُّشْفِقُونَ

Verily those who live in awe for fear of their Lord" (Qur'an 23:57).

In order to stop unnatural fears and worry about the consequences of one's own action, one has to make sure to live decently without wrongdoing and follow the equilateral triangle of relationships between theo-ethics, socio-ethics, and psycho-ethics. In order to avoid any fear, we need to know that the chart of an equilateral triangle where all three sides are equal. The top is theo-ethics, and the bottom right and left are socio- ethics and psycho ethics. Both bottom relationships lead to theo-ethics, and He is the source of mercy and forgiveness. Although, all angles are equal and they are reflective of each other. The mid-segment of a triangle is the theo-ethics response to both socio-ethics and psycho ethics, which is the reflection given to both bases.

THE NATURE OF GOD IN ISLAM

The core principle of Islamic life is the presence, existence, and acceptance of God in our minds. Before we discuss the role of God in human affairs, we have to understand the meaning of God in Islam literally. "Allah" comes from the Arabic word "elah" a God or something to be worshiped. This world (Elah) can be made plural (Gods), as in "Aleha" and it can be male or female just as the word in English can be "Goddess". "Allah" has no gender, not male or female. "He" is used only out of respect and dignity-not for gender. Allah is always singular, never plural. "We" is only used as the "Royal We" just as in English for royalty. ³ Allah means "The only One that can be worshiped". God, in the Qur'an defines Himself on Chapter 112ᵗʰ saying,

قُلْ هُوَ ٱللَّهُ أَحَدٌ (١) ٱللَّهُ ٱلصَّمَدُ (٢) لَمْ يَلِدْ وَلَمْ يُولَدْ (٣) وَلَمْ يَكُن لَّهُ كُفُوًا أَحَدٌ (٤

"He is God the One and Only God, the Eternal, Absolute, He begetteth not, nor is He begotten, and there is none like unto Him."

According to Abdullah Yusuf Ali, the most famous interpreter of the Qur'an in the English language, we read, "We are taught to avoid the pitfalls into which men and women and nations have fallen at various times in trying to understand God. We have to note that His nature is so sublime, so far beyond our limited conception, that the best way in which we can realize Him is to feel that He is a Personality."

The late Al-Faruqi in his very comprehensive book, *"Tawhid": It's implications for taught in life*, we read:

"Where God is not merely an absolute, ultimate first cause of principle but a core of normativeness. It is this aspect of God that suffers most in any theory where God becomes a *deus otiousus;* and it is the Muslim's responsiveness to this core of normativeness that the philosopher's theory throws out of joint/ God as normativeness means that He is the Being Who command. His movements, thoughts, and deeds are all realities beyond doubt; but everyone of these, in so far as man conceives of it, is for him a value, an ought-to-be, even when, in the case where it is already realized, no ought-to-do flows from it. Besides being metaphysical, God's ultimacy is not for the Muslim isolable from, or to be emphasizable at the cost of the axiological". [4]

God, in Islam, is the first causal of principle, the beginning and the end. As well as the Unique One; He does not resemble anyone, because He does not exist in human form. God is all knowing, all wise, and He has given the world an order and He keeps that order. He constantly watches His creation and He recreates His creations as He deems necessary for ecological survival. The oneness of God has a vast meaning philosophically, socially, and psychologically, including that He is the core principle of all vital existence on Earth. Belief in God is what makes a Muslim a Muslim; they must believe in Him totality, not partially. Man resorts to God for guidance when and where the human understanding fails. God is the Lawgiver and has the final say in what matters. Having said that, the law of nature and the law of Allah, are the one and the same. Karen Armstrong, author of *A History of God*, writes:

"In the Koran, however, Al-Lah is more impersonal than YHWH. He lacks the pathos and passion of the biblical God. We can only glimpse something of God in the "signs" of nature and so transcendent is he that we can only talk about him in "parables". Constantly, therefore, the Koran urges Muslims to see the world as an epiphany; they must make the imaginative effort to see *through* the fragmentary world to the full power of original being, to the transcendent reality that infuses all things." [5]

Psychologically, believing in God, means that there is direct relationship between mankind and God. Mankind does not see Him, but they feel His existence. Mankind knows that God sees them, that God hears them, that God knows the secret of their hearts. All this tells us is that mankind is not alone. God is with mankind 24/7, asleep, and awake. Although God constantly watches over mankind, mankind also has the free will to obey Him or not to obey Him. As with, we choose to be, to be guided or not to be guided. One thing that is certain is that the more mankind remembers God, the more peace of mind will come to him. This is only true with total submission. The role of God, on humanity, is to guide mankind in felicity and light because God, according to the Qur'an, is the source of all things that may happen. The Qur'an says,

ثُمَّ أَنزَلَ عَلَيْكُم مِّنْ بَعْدِ ٱلْغَمِّ أَمَنَةً نُّعَاسًا يَغْشَىٰ طَآئِفَةً مِّنكُمْ ۖ وَطَآئِفَةٌ قَدْ أَهَمَّتْهُمْ أَنفُسُهُمْ يَظُنُّونَ بِٱللَّهِ غَيْرَ ٱلْحَقِّ ظَنَّ ٱلْجَٰهِلِيَّةِ ۖ يَقُولُونَ هَل لَّنَا مِنَ ٱلْأَمْرِ مِن شَىْءٍ ۗ قُلْ إِنَّ ٱلْأَمْرَ كُلَّهُ لِلَّهِ ۗ يُخْفُونَ فِىٓ أَنفُسِهِم مَّا لَا يُبْدُونَ لَكَ ۖ يَقُولُونَ لَوْ كَانَ لَنَا مِنَ ٱلْأَمْرِ شَىْءٌ مَّا قُتِلْنَا هَٰهُنَا ۗ قُل لَّوْ كُنتُمْ فِى بُيُوتِكُمْ لَبَرَزَ ٱلَّذِينَ كُتِبَ عَلَيْهِمُ ٱلْقَتْلُ إِلَىٰ مَضَاجِعِهِمْ ۖ وَلِيَبْتَلِىَ ٱللَّهُ مَا فِى صُدُورِكُمْ وَلِيُمَحِّصَ مَا فِى قُلُوبِكُمْ ۗ وَٱللَّهُ عَلِيمٌ بِذَاتِ ٱلصُّدُورِ

"After (the excitement) of the distress, He sent down calm on a band of you overcome with slumber, while another band was stirred to anxiety by their own feelings, moved by wrong suspicions due to ignorance. They said, "What affair is this of ours?" Say thou: "Indeed, this affair is wholly of God's." They hide in their minds what they dare not reveal to thee" (Quran 3:154).

The relationship between an individual and his Creator is very personal. There is no intercession or mediation between mankind and his Creator, because the only being that knows mankind's heart and mind is the Creator Himself. There is no one else who has access to another person's heart or mind but themselves and the Creator. Those who do wrong, means they have taken God out of their hearts, deliberately. If people do wrong, that does not mean that God is unjust, but people do wrong on themselves. The intention of God and mankind is nothing but goodwill.

Mankind can commit wrong out of their own evil desires, but return back to their Creator for forgiveness and mercy because He is the source of mercy. According to Islam, God is infinity and beyond, and the minds of humans, though physically finite, are very vast. Our minds have the capacity to reach higher goals without any limitation, but if they do one thing wrong, they are accountable for it and if they do one thing right, they get rewarded for it. The understanding of God, in relationship to mankind, leads to the philosophy of Tawhid, the oneness of God.

TAWHID: ONENESS OF GOD

The oneness of God is the principle of *Tawhid*, with God as one, universe as one, mankind as one, and knowledge as one. All of these originate from one God alone, Allah. According to the renown Muslim sociologist of the 20th century, Ali Shariati, he explains Tawhid as "Regarding the whole cosmos as a unity instead of diving it into this world into the hereafter, the natural and the supernatural, substance and meaning, spirit and body. It means regarding the whole as an existence as a single, living form in a conscience organism. Possessing will, intelligence, feeling, and purpose". [6]

Tawhid is a worldview. It gives a person direction, achievement, purpose, a goal and an objective in life. Tawhid gives hope, because the ultimate hope for success and achievement is to return to God. Mankind's responsibility towards Tawhid is to align all of their actions to achieve and reach to God. Because of this principle, Islam is the complete way of life and encompasses all aspects of life. Therefore, a Muslim cannot be detached from politics, economics, and social life in continuous learning. Tawhid is the totality of life and it is only though Tawhid that the ideal world system will be achieved. Since human beings are accountable in the Hereafter, they have to be sure that their agenda in life is to please God and mankind. This means that human beings are not only responsible for themselves, but are responsible to take charge. The Qur'an says,

إِنَّا عَرَضْنَا ٱلْأَمَانَةَ عَلَى ٱلسَّمَٰوَٰتِ وَٱلْأَرْضِ وَٱلْجِبَالِ فَأَبَيْنَ أَن يَحْمِلْنَهَا وَأَشْفَقْنَ مِنْهَا وَحَمَلَهَا ٱلْإِنسَٰنُ إِنَّهُ كَانَ ظَلُومًا جَهُولًا

"Mankind accepted responsibility for this expectation: indeed we offer the trust of volitional faith to the heavens and the earth in the mountains. But they refused to bear it and were fearful of it. Yet, the human being bore it" (Quran 33:72).

Tawhid rejects any sort of duality, trinity, or multiplicity. The course of the whole creation of God; He is the one that makes things happen. He is the source of knowledge and wisdom. Human beings learn from Him. God teaches humans through His natural law to be productive, cooperative, and a meaningful member of a social system. Tawhid gives people direction, vision, a worldview, and the principles of living. This idea also makes them civilized, because God knows in what ways His creation should perform to reach their potential. Tawhid is the gateway through science and knowledge and it is through this gateway, that mankind will reach mental stability and eventually felicity, because tawhid aligns all orders with the natural law. Tawhid is not a man-made philosophy or theory. Tawhid is a divine principle of entities, mankind included. Without tawhid, human beings are like astronauts, floating in outer space without a solid ground for human beings to settle on. Tawhid has not been designed for Muslims only, it has also been formulated and composed for humanity as one body. Tawhid rejects any sort of discrimination, biases, and prejudices but at the same time establishes justice for all without making human beings as servants to one another but to God only. Tawhid not only bonds mankind to God, but bonds mankind to nature as well. Tawhid stands against corruption, constantly reminding humanity of their responsibility to the Earth. The Qur'an says,

بَلْ أَتَيْنَٰهُم بِذِكْرِهِمْ فَهُمْ عَن ذِكْرِهِم مُّعْرِضُونَ

"Rather, We have brought them the Quran to be their revealed reminder of the way of God. Yet, they turn away from the guidance of their revealed reminder" (Quran 23:71).

Only those who understand, see, and comprehend tawhid use this intelligence to discover the universality of His creations. This universality means that the whole natural system, mankind included, is running an operation from one main source and that main source is Allah. The Qur'an says,

وَهُوَ ٱلَّذِىٓ أَنشَأَ لَكُمُ ٱلسَّمْعَ وَٱلْأَبْصَرَ وَٱلْأَفْئِدَةَ قَلِيلًا مَّا تَشْكُرُونَ

"Yet He alone is the One who has brought fourth all of you human beings the facilities of hearing, sight, and hearts, that comprehend, how little thanks that you give" (Quran 23:78).

God is One, because the whole cosmos are one and everything in it, is therefore, interrelated. All are submissive to the natural law and the source is Allah. That is the essence of submission to Allah. When a Muslim says submission to the will of Allah, it is not a fatalist statement but it is a scientific fact that has to be understood in accordance to the Qur'an that we are all part of the cosmic system governed by natural laws. Our responsibility as human beings, is to use our intelligence effectively for our own growth, safety, and wellbeing without jeopardizing our own mental existence and without compromising the most valuable gift from God, which is "A'ql" (intelligence). Tawhid is the essence of living for humanity that includes all aspects of life without hesitation.

The genetic makeup of DNA can be found in both plants and humans, which begins in the formation of the "double helix". DNA in vegetation and human beings share the same genetics base pairs and "ACGT", which accounts for protein that exists in our bodies and governs function for living properties. DNA is built of nucleotides: adenine, cytosine, guanine, and thymine. These genetic codes that are stored, with DNA, express a sequence that dictates the form in plants, animals, and human beings. DNA is a common thread that connects all living organisms, which is why we conclude that tawhid, the Law of Nature and Law of Allah, are one and the same.

Understanding this fact, that Law of Nature and Law of Allah are one and the same, and understanding the fact, scientifically, that the DNA in other creations can be found in humans, makes us reach a conclusion about monotheism that not only is there one God, but the whole universal system, mankind included, is one.

According to the Qur'an, Prophet Abraham was neither a Jew nor a Christian, but was a monotheist, believing in one God and submitted to God's will."The word Monotheist (Hanif) describes a person who follows the "true religion". This is deep-rooted within the self in the nature originated by God—submission to God's will. This submission in the monotheist is absolute and the antithesis of worshiping more than one God. To be a monotheist, is to have the desire and inclination towards the Truth, the Real". [7] A monotheistic person is one who sees themselves within the orbit of the unity of existence.

To reach the level of monotheism is to comprehend and conceive the reality of monotheism as one whole entity and recognize that the One who created us, is One and that comes through *Iman.* "Iman is not merely an ethical category. Indeed it is firstly a cognitive category: that is to say it has to do with knowledge. With the truthfulness of its prepositions. In essence that nature of its propositional content is that of first principle of logic and knowledge, of metaphysics, of ethics, and aesthetics, it follows that in acts in the subject as a light with illuminates everything". [8]

One of the problems of chaos and disaster within humanity reflected in the lifestyles of individuals, the communities, and nations is that even those who claim to be monotheistic, claiming to know one God, still have not reached the potential of understanding their responsibilities as a monotheist towards the self and the natural law. This means, that just following the rituals of religion, such as prayer or fasting does not automatically make us a true monotheist. A monotheist is the one who submits to the will of God and aligns all the affairs according to the Law of Nature and the Law of God. According to the Qur'an, the whole universe is created with perfect moderation and measurement.

An individual has to adjust their lifestyle to be moderate at any level in different situations in life and to be aligned with the natural law. Anything that can put a human being out of balance, in an ordinary situation, means they are out of the monotheistic orbit. As a result, "they foster operation, discrimination, prejudice, intolerance, and injustice, this ignorance manifest itself in certain cognitive, effective, and behavioral patterns which are clearly evident of them having forgotten their original nature, their heart, their covenant with their Lord, their being potentially the trustee of nature, and God's vicegerent on earth".[9]

Psychologically speaking, a mindset of a monotheist and their mental attitude, is designed to not only align with the Law of Nature but also please their Creator at the same time. This is the felicity of this world and the Hereafter for a pure monotheist individual. As we said above, a pure monotheist who submits to the will of God, and aligns his/her thoughts based on monotheism, shuns away from all sorts of radicalism and "fundamentalism". A monotheist is engulfed with peace and serenity for himself/herself and others.

Monotheism is not only a psychological principle but also a total worldview for existence. A monotheistic mind creates things in a living style that suits a total balance within the social system. To do that, they have to perform justice in all matters of life. As we said earlier, *"A'dl"*, which means justice applied to all aspects of life, not only for the judicial system. For example, eating in moderation, sleeping in moderation, working in moderation, and taking care of others in moderation are all examples of applications of monotheism in daily life.

As noted earlier, Tawhid, monotheism, stands on the concept of God alone. According to the Qur'an, God created mankind to serve Him, *Ibada*, worship. However, it has a broader application within Islamic life in monotheism. Worship means total obedience of Allah. The epicenter of all things that happen; He is the cause of all good things and has made human beings as His vicegerent on Earth. In Islam or any other monotheistic religions, worship does not mean to just pray or meditate. The Qur'an says,

وقُل رَّبِّ زِدْنِى عِلْمًا

"Oh my lord, advance me knowledge" (Qur'an 20:114).

This means that it is our responsibility to constantly learn because we cannot achieve our goal without striving for knowledge and actually learning. We obey by learning and seeking knowledge and by doing this we are also worshiping Him. Another example is that Allah asks us to refrain from anger, when we do that, we not only become at peace with ourselves but by obeying this command of Allah, we are worshiping Him. The Qur'an clearly says,

ٱلَّذِينَ يُنفِقُونَ فِى ٱلسَّرَّآءِ وَٱلضَّرَّآءِ وَٱلْكَـٰظِمِينَ ٱلْغَيْظَ
وَٱلْعَافِينَ عَنِ ٱلنَّاسِ وَٱللَّهُ يُحِبُّ ٱلْمُحْسِنِينَ

"Who suppress their rage, and who pardon people for God loves those who excel in doing good" (Qur'an, 3:134).

If we look closely in the field of monotheism and oneness of the universe and of mankind, we reach to a conclusion that Islam disregards anything in life that are separated and not unified. Lack of unity is not aligned with monotheism.

CREATION OF MANKIND IN ISLAM

It is important that we focus about the creation of human beings in Islam, because the whole psychology of mankind is based upon behaviorism, humanism, psycho-dynamic, bio-psychology, and cognitive psychology. What defines human beings, as the most distinguished creation on Earth, by God, is his mental capability and power.

According to Islam, mankind has been created free; both male and female are created from a single soul and the Qur'an talks about creation of humankind by saying,

يَٰٓأَيُّهَا ٱلنَّاسُ ٱتَّقُواْ رَبَّكُمُ ٱلَّذِى خَلَقَكُم مِّن نَّفْسٍ وَٰحِدَةٍ
وَخَلَقَ مِنْهَا زَوْجَهَا وَبَثَّ مِنْهُمَا رِجَالًا كَثِيرًا وَنِسَآءً
وَٱتَّقُواْ ٱللَّهَ ٱلَّذِى تَسَآءَلُونَ بِهِۦ وَٱلْأَرْحَامَ إِنَّ ٱللَّهَ كَانَ عَلَيْكُمْ رَقِيبًا

"Oh mankind! Reverence your guardian-Lord, who created you from a single person created, of like nature, his mate and from them twain scattered (like seeds) countless men and women; reverence God, through Whom ye demand your mutual (rights), and (reverence) the whom that bore you: for God ever watches over you" (Qur'an 4:1).

This verse from a bio-psychology point of view, rejects the theory that men and women are different intellectually, learning capacity, intelligence, and instinct. This verse clearly implies that there are no duality and discrimination in creation between men and women. There are more verses in the Qur'an that support the equal creation of men and women:

لَقَدْ خَلَقْنَا ٱلْإِنسَـٰنَ فِىٓ أَحْسَنِ تَقْوِيمٍ

"We have indeed created man in the best of molds" (Qur'an 95:4).

Again, this verse alludes to the fact that there are no distinctions between men and women.

The following verses supports the theory of the creation of mankind from a biological point of view. Chapter 75 (resurrection) verses 37, 38, and 39 proves the biological creation as follows:

أَلَمْ يَكُ نُطْفَةً مِّن مَّنِىٍّ يُمْنَىٰ (٣٧)
ثُمَّ كَانَ عَلَقَةً فَخَلَقَ فَسَوَّىٰ (٣٨)
فَجَعَلَ مِنْهُ ٱلزَّوْجَيْنِ ٱلذَّكَرَ وَٱلْأُنثَىٰٓ (٣٩)

Verse 37: "Was he not a drop of sperm emitted (in lowly form)"

Verse 38: "Then did he become a leeched-like clot: then did (God) make and fashion him in due proportion"

Verse 39: "And of Him He made two sexes, male and female"

Since Law of Nature and Law of God are one and the same, then, mankind is a natural entity. The Qur'an says,

وَإِلَىٰ ثَمُودَ أَخَاهُمْ صَـٰلِحًا قَالَ يَـٰقَوْمِ ٱعْبُدُوا۟ ٱللَّهَ مَا لَكُم مِّنْ إِلَـٰهٍ غَيْرُهُۥ هُوَ أَنشَأَكُم مِّنَ ٱلْأَرْضِ وَٱسْتَعْمَرَكُمْ فِيهَا فَٱسْتَغْفِرُوهُ ثُمَّ تُوبُوٓا۟ إِلَيْهِ إِنَّ رَبِّى قَرِيبٌ مُّجِيبٌ

"God speaks to the people of Thamud "(We sent) Salih, one of their own brethren. He said: "O my People! Worship God: ye have no other God but Him, It is He who had produced you from the Earth and settled you therein" (Qur'an 11:61).

The Qur'an also speaks not only about the human creation but ontology, the creation from birth to death.

يَـٰٓأَيُّهَا ٱلنَّاسُ إِن كُنتُمْ فِى رَيْبٍ مِّنَ ٱلْبَعْثِ فَإِنَّا خَلَقْنَـٰكُم مِّن تُرَابٍ ثُمَّ مِن نُّطْفَةٍ
ثُمَّ مِنْ عَلَقَةٍ ثُمَّ مِن مُّضْغَةٍ مُّخَلَّقَةٍ وَغَيْرِ مُخَلَّقَةٍ لِّنُبَيِّنَ لَكُمْ وَنُقِرُّ فِى ٱلْأَرْحَامِ مَا
نَشَآءُ إِلَىٰٓ أَجَلٍ مُّسَمًّى ثُمَّ نُخْرِجُكُمْ طِفْلًا ثُمَّ لِتَبْلُغُوٓا۟ أَشُدَّكُمْ وَمِنكُم مَّن يُتَوَفَّىٰ
وَمِنكُم مَّن يُرَدُّ إِلَىٰٓ أَرْذَلِ ٱلْعُمُرِ لِكَيْلَا يَعْلَمَ مِنۢ بَعْدِ عِلْمٍ شَيْـًٔا وَتَرَى ٱلْأَرْضَ
هَامِدَةً فَإِذَآ أَنزَلْنَا عَلَيْهَا ٱلْمَآءَ ٱهْتَزَّتْ وَرَبَتْ وَأَنۢبَتَتْ مِن كُلِّ زَوْجٍۭ بَهِيجٍ

"Oh mankind! If ye have a doubt about the Resurrection, (consider) that
We created you out of dust, then out of sperm, then out of a leech-like
clot, then out of a morsel of flesh, partly unformed, in order that We
may manifest (our power) to you; and We cause whom We will to rest
in the wombs for an appointed term, then do We bring you out as babes,
then (foster you) that ye may reach your age of full strength; and some
of you are called to die. And some are sent back to the feeblest old age,
so that they know nothing after having known (much). And (further),
thou seest the earth barren and lifeless, but when We pour down rain on
it, it is stirred (to life), it swells, and it puts forth every kind of beautiful
growth (in pairs)". (Qur'an 22:5).

The above verses clearly pinpoint the fact that men and women are
natural entities and according to the Law of Nature, they are created
the same and are part of the natural system. Both men and women are
created in the best form and moderation; they have the same spiritual
and intellectual balance in their creation.

The only thing that we have to pay attention is that the brain of a
woman is slightly smaller (physiologically) than the brain of a man.
The Qur'an says,

وَلِلرِّجَالِ عَلَيْهِنَّ دَرَجَةٌ

"But men have a degree (of advantage) over them (women)" (Qur'an
2:228).

Here, the term "degree" actually is a mathematical term that scientifically
implies to the size of the brain, not overall, advantage of men over

women. In many of the interpretations of the Qur'an and almost all of the interpretations of the Qur'an, this "degree" has been misinterpreted as an overall economic, social, political, and intelligence of men over women which does not correspond to the previous verses that we quoted about creation. The intelligence quotient of both men and women are the same based upon the above verses. However, the argument comes to the question as to why some people are smarter than others. Is this because there is a difference in intelligence? The answer to this is that God has created every human being with a specific talent and intelligence. At the same time, individuals have different interests in life. For example, we have two students in class, the same age, same gender, the same socioeconomic status, race, but one gets ahead compared to the other boy. The reason is that one who gets ahead, has a different interest, motivation, and objective in life. This does not mean that the other boy is less intelligent. The other one, student B, put less time and effort and is not exploring his abilities to achieve his goal. That is why the Prophet of Islam says "Those who know themselves, know God".

Men and women have the same mental capability and power, the Qur'an says,

فَٱسْتَجَابَ لَهُمْ رَبُّهُمْ أَنِّى لَا أُضِيعُ عَمَلَ عَٰمِلٍ مِّنكُم مِّن ذَكَرٍ أَوْ أُنثَىٰ ۖ بَعْضُكُم مِّنۢ بَعْضٍ ۖ

"Never will I suffer to be lost the work of any of you, be a male or female: You are members one of another" (Qur'an 3:195).

NATURE VS. NURTURE

The definition of nature and nurture is that nature theorizes our behavior and personality is influenced by biological factors and gene inheritance, whereas nurture insists that behavior and personality are influenced by environmental factors. When we study nature, we face a monumental task, which is finding out how far we could go to trace the gene. This means that whatever are factors of malfunction biologically and behaviorally in a person, we blame it on genetic inheritances. This is our argument against this theory. According to the Qur'an, mankind has been created on earth in the best of molds. The combination of the two, earth and mold, gives us the logic that there is nothing wrong in the creation of mankind from the very beginning. However, we cannot deny the impact of the environmental factors that can easily influence us biologically and behaviorally, such as social pressures, tyranny, economic aspects, or even malnutrition that eventually affects and infects the fittest, or even a person born because of wrongdoings of ourselves and from others.

There is some truth to the debate of nature vs. nurture. It has been known for a very long time that our physical characteristics are determined biologically; our eye, hair, and skin color, our features, the diseases that we inherit, and even life expectancy, are all genetically inherited. The debate of nature versus nurture brings up the idea that our behavior and mental abilities are also wired into our biology, from our genetic inheritance. This idea that the behavior and mental abilities are also genetically inherited is completely wrong. A thief will not reproduce a thief and that is logically not acceptable because a civic behavior requires a strong leadership, economic security, safety, and the total wellbeing of an individual from environmental factors starting from the parents because they can have the most influence of how the child will turn out to be. Going back to the idea of a thief reproducing a thief, unless a thief's child is exposed to this constant behavior of stealing, the child will believe that this behavior is acceptable in society and will continue to follow the footsteps of the parent who is a thief.

From day one of birth, Islam takes into consideration the issue of nurture even before birth and that is the principle of *rahma* (compassion) meaning that before birth, the surrounding family members should have *rahma,* which constitutes kindness, care, support, and compassion without any hesitation to the carrying mother. This will secure the mental stability of the mother, which eventually affects the fetus. The mental stability of the mother during pregnancy is very important because if her stability is unstable, it could affect the fetus in the long run. A study conducted at the University of California-Irvine by Curt A. Sandman, Elysia P. Davis, and Laura M. Glynn studied how the mother's psychological state affects a developing fetus. Their research focused mainly on pregnant women with depression, either before or after birth. The research found that "In the long term, having a depressed mother could lead to neurological problems and psychiatric disorders, Sandman says. In another study, his team found that older children whose mothers were anxious during pregnancy, which often is comorbid with depression, have differences in certain brain structures. It will take studies lasting decades to figure out exactly what having a depressed mother means to a child's long-term health". [10]

BEHAVIORISM

Behaviorism is the study of overt and observable behavior. This is the most important of Islamic psychology because observable behavior determines a person's personality within the social system. In Islam, how one behaves is based upon the role modeling of the Prophet of Islam and his noble family. The Qur'an clearly says that the Prophet is a role model of conduct. All Prophets, according to Islam, came to this world for two main reasons: to worship the one and only God, and make people moral and ethical. The psychological impact of Muhammad's behavior on a true faithful Muslim is enormous. This is because behavior, character, and personality of an individual, being male or female, are formulated by the behavior of the Prophet and his noble family. The Qur'an says,

لَّقَدْ كَانَ لَكُمْ فِى رَسُولِ ٱللَّهِ أُسْوَةٌ حَسَنَةٌ لِّمَن كَانَ يَرْجُواْ ٱللَّهَ وَٱلْيَوْمَ ٱلْأَخِرَ وَذَكَرَ ٱللَّهَ كَثِيرًا

"We have indeed in the Messenger of Allah, a beautiful pattern (in conduct) (Qur'an 33:21).

This means he was a noble man and had the highest moral standing. It is important for Muslims to learn the proper behavior from Prophet Muhammad and apply it in their daily lives. So behaviorism in Islam is not something that is formulated by outside forces coming from unknown sources or irrationally. Misconduct in behavior, according to Islamic psychology, means that the individual is not following the footstep of his master. All wrongdoings, atrocities, and abuses committed by a Muslim are because they are out of touch with their master.

Islamic behaviorism must be aligned with natural phenomenon-that a man is created with free will and a mindset. In this case, we can condition a mind by training specific things, but at the same time the mind has the power to shift, change, and reject at any time it wants. Conditioning, as most behavioral psychologist emphasize, could actually be very unconditional because of the latitude of the mind. The difference between the man and the animal structure of the brain in the mind is that it is given to mankind as a gift. The Qur'an says,

أَفَلَا يَتَدَبَّرُونَ ٱلْقُرْءَانَ أَمْ عَلَىٰ قُلُوبٍ أَقْفَالُهَآ

"Do they not then earnestly seek to understand the Qur'an, or are their hearts locked up by them". (Qur'an 47:24).

This means that this is the thinking mode of human mind that makes it unconditional to condition like animals. Besides, alongside intelligence and the different mindset, God gives mankind His own spirit, which is why according to Aristotle, humans are hylo-morphic, that, is mankind is made from corpse and spirit. Spirit is part of the mind; there is no scientific proof that animals possess spirit. They may have intelligence and emotion that distinguishes their instinct desire. The Qur'an says,

ثُمَّ سَوَّىٰهُ وَنَفَخَ فِيهِ مِن رُّوحِهِۦ وَجَعَلَ لَكُمُ ٱلسَّمْعَ وَٱلْأَبْصَٰرَ وَٱلْأَفْـِٔدَةَ قَلِيلًا مَّا تَشْكُرُونَ

"But He fashioned him in due proportion, and he breathed into him something of His spirit. And He gave you (the faculties of) hearing and sight and feeling (and understanding): little thanks do ye give". (Quran 32:9).

One thing that is very important to note that God is infinity and the mind of the human being is also vast. The mind can reach very high levels but is also limited. So far, no one knows about his or her true nature of spirit. There is no scientific proof of spirit that humankind possesses. The Qur'an says,

وَيَسْـَٔلُونَكَ عَنِ ٱلرُّوحِ قُلِ ٱلرُّوحُ مِنْ أَمْرِ رَبِّى وَمَآ أُوتِيتُم مِّنَ ٱلْعِلْمِ إِلَّا قَلِيلًا

"They ask thee concerning the spirit (of inspiration) say: 'The Spirit (cometh) by command of my Lord: of knowledge it is only a little that is communicated to you, (O men!)". (Qur'an 17:85).

THE JEWELS OF THE HEART

Our actions are based upon our *niyah,* intention. Jewels of the heart are building blocks of personality and of a believer. How we utilize our heart for the right path is on our hands. Jewels of the heart are the gems that make our hearts the most valuable epicenter of our life. As we mentioned earlier, there are good qualities and bad qualities that a human being can possess. Our challenge is to keep up with the good qualities and diminish bad qualities in order to be a person with dignity and integrity. The following are gems of heart that needs extra attention to not be rusted.

1) **Polishing the heart by *Zikr* (remembrance of Allah)** –Remembrance of Allah must become a habit to make sure that our heart is not getting polluted. If human beings, according to Islam, forget Allah, Allah will forget them and that is the most dangerous psychological aspect of human life when one does not polish the heart and forgets Allah.

2) **Purification of the heart** – By purifying the heart, we mean to do good things such as paying charity, helping and supporting others. In order to keep the heart pure, one has to stay away from any factors that displease Allah.

3) **Tender Hearted-** In order to keep the heart tender and caring, a Muslim should recite the Qur'an. It is understood that Qur'an

has the power to make hearts compassionate. The best example is the story of 'Umar Ibn Al- Khattâb. He was angry at his sister for reciting the Qur'an and asked his sister what she was reading and as a response to that question, she recited the Qur'an to him. It is narrated that that recitation from his sister not only changed his heart but his life.

4) **Firmness in belief of Islam** - A weak belief will mislead the individual and cause him distress and hopelessness. On the contrary, a strong belief in Allah, his commands, and the maxims of the Prophet lead him to prosperity and success. According to Islamic psychology, people go astray because they make continuous mistakes. Not because they're not talented, but because they're weak in their faith. The Qur'an says, "Oh my lord, Advance me in knowledge!" (Qur'an 20:114). So this command is for individual growth and success and if he fails, it means that he's not committed to that verse in the Qur'an.

5) **Performing Salat**- Salat (prayers) is another gem of the heart. The difference between Salat and Zikr is that Salat is performed five times a day while Zikr is continuous 24 hours by remembering Him, glorifying His name, thanking Him for the bounties, etc. The importance of Salat, according to the Qur'an, that makes a person stay away from wrongdoing and at the same time burns the mistakes we do between one Salat and the next and keeps the heart pure of any wrongdoing and pollution.

6) **Stay away from Haram**- Anything that is prohibited by Allah in the form of actions or eating can pollute the heart such as eating pork meat or drinking alcoholic beverages. Since there is a direct connection between the heart and the mind, prohibited intake will damage the mind and pollute the heart.

7) **Disbelieving in superstitions, omens, fortune-telling, etc.**- These destruct the universality of Tawhid (Oneness of God). Humans tend to forget that all sources of good is Allah. Resorting

to any other being than Allah is derailing himself from the right path because instead of trusting Allah, he relies on other beings who are not eternal.

8) **Having strong listening and learning skills**- Only those will be guided that they listen, obey, and apply to their lives.

9) **Humility**- Gem of the heart that no one should think that he is superior than one another and must see himself equal to others. It is only his responsibility that counts not his social status, wealth, race, or even language.

10) **Avoid Complaining**- This does not mean that one should not rise for his rights when oppressed; it means social complaining that people have unnecessary expectations from others including family members.

PATIENCE IS A VIRTUE

An important psychological aspect of faith is to have patience when dealing with a variety of circumstances and calamities. Patience is different in Islamic culture but before we deal with different kinds of patience, it is important that we refer to some verses regarding patience. The Qur'an says,

وَٱلْعَصْرِ (١)
إِنَّ ٱلْإِنسَٰنَ لَفِى خُسْرٍ (٢)
إِلَّا ٱلَّذِينَ ءَامَنُواْ وَعَمِلُواْ ٱلصَّٰلِحَٰتِ وَتَوَاصَوْاْ بِٱلْحَقِّ وَتَوَاصَوْاْ بِٱلصَّبْرِ (٣)

"By the token of time through the ages",

"Verily man is in loss"

"Except such as has faith and do righteous deeds and join together in the mutual teaching of truth and of patience and constancy" (Qur'an 103:1-3).

Also, the Qur'an says,

يَٰأَيُّهَا ٱلَّذِينَ ءَامَنُواْ ٱسْتَعِينُواْ بِٱلصَّبْرِ وَٱلصَّلَوٰةِ إِنَّ ٱللَّهَ مَعَ ٱلصَّٰبِرِينَ

"O you who have believe, seek help through patience and prayers. Indeed, Allah is with the patient" (Qur'an 2:153).

In the above verses, God has emphasized by time saying that mankind is going to be in a state of loss if they waste time not doing the right things. Most importantly, faith has been connected with righteous deeds and that is teaching the truth and to be steadfast on the true path with patience so one could see the results. Hereby, we can clearly see that patience without being steadfast in the right path is a waste of time and energy. At the same time, patience without deep conviction to the principles of *Tawhid* is a waste of time and energy. A man must be patient and must avoid any disturbances of the mind to see the results of his righteous deed. This is because mankind cannot foresee a lot of things about their life. For example, a person at the age of twenty cannot truly see what will happen to him twenty years later. So things may happen that are beyond a human's control such as catastrophes, an illness, or death; these natural disasters are not in control of mankind so one has to practice patience, which could be a trial of worldly life. In many instances, people do not know what is really truly good for them, and it is at this stage, that patience is a virtue. For example, one has an appointment at some specific time but before reaching that appointment, he gets a flat tire. He sees that incident as a bad accident. But, that may be good for him that his flat tire may have prevented a major accident five minutes ahead. The Qur'an says,

وَعَسَىٰٓ أَن تَكۡرَهُواْ شَيۡـًٔا وَهُوَ خَيۡرٌ لَّكُمۡۖ وَعَسَىٰٓ أَن تُحِبُّواْ شَيۡـًٔا وَهُوَ شَرٌّ لَّكُمۡۚ وَٱللَّهُ يَعۡلَمُ وَأَنتُمۡ لَا تَعۡلَمُونَ

"But it is possible that you dislike a thing which is good for you and that you love a thing which is bad for you but God knows and you know not" (Qur'an 2:216).

At any event, a person of faith should ask for his *khair*, (good), from Allah. At the same time, practice patience and resort to prayers and supplications; we have to be constant in doing the right thing for achieving our goal. With Allah's help and support, if a person is not doing the right thing, that will cost them failure even if they pray and offer supplications because prayers and supplications are associated with good work and vice versa. If a student does not study, fails a test, and truly believes that failing that test was his destiny, then he is wrong. That is not his destiny because he made failure his destiny by not studying. One has to strive with the help of Allah to achieve goals by being patient and by understanding that efforts alone may not be as fruitful as one might think.

There are three kinds of patience:

Patience of *Mussibah*: Calamities and bad accidents occurring to someone that are not in his control. The Qur'an says,

ٱلَّذِينَ إِذَآ أَصَٰبَتْهُم مُّصِيبَةٌ قَالُوٓاْ إِنَّا لِلَّهِ وَإِنَّآ إِلَيْهِ رَٰجِعُونَ

"Who, when calamity befalls them, say, "verily, unto God do we belong and, verily, unto Him we shall return" (Qur'an 2:156).

Patience of *Ibada*: When one has enough patience to worship Allah to avoid committing sin and stay constantly on the right path and achieve *nafs mutma-inna,* that is the soul at rest/peace. The Qur'an says,

أَصْبِرْ وَمَا صَبْرُكَ إِلَّا بِٱللَّهِ وَلَا تَحْزَنْ عَلَيْهِمْ وَلَا تَكُ فِى ضَيْقٍ مِّمَّا يَمْكُرُونَ

"And be patience, (O Muhammad), and your patience is not but through Allah. And do not grieve over them and do not be in distress over what they conspire" (Qur'an 16:127).

Patience of *Nimah*: When a person is granted a lot of good things but he loses patience and is ungrateful and forgets Allah Who provided all of this, and eventually becomes selfish, forgetful, boastful and thus impatient. The Qur'an says,

وَمَن يُبَدِّلْ نِعْمَةَ ٱللَّهِ مِنْ بَعْدِ مَا جَآءَتْهُ فَإِنَّ ٱللَّهَ شَدِيدُ ٱلْعِقَابِ

"And whoever exchanges the favor of Allah (for disbelief) after it has come to him-then indeed, Allah is severe in penalty" (Qur'an 2:211).

Patience of *Darar*: When a person is committed to his work and does all the right things but at the same time incurs a loss. *Khair* (good) in this loss. The Qur'an says,

إِن تَمْسَسْكُمْ حَسَنَةٌ تَسُؤْهُمْ وَإِن تُصِبْكُمْ سَيِّئَةٌ يَفْرَحُواْ بِهَا ۖ
وَإِن تَصْبِرُواْ وَتَتَّقُواْ لَا يَضُرُّكُمْ كَيْدُهُمْ شَيْئًا
إِنَّ اللَّهَ بِمَا يَعْمَلُونَ مُحِيطٌ

"If good touches you, it distresses them; but if harm strikes you, they rejoice it. And if you are patient and fear Allah, their plot will not harm you at all. Indeed, Allah is encompassing what they do" (Qur'an 3:120).

Yusuf Ali writes about the above verse, "God's helps come to those who strive with firmness, as it did at Badr. Much can be learned from the misfortunes at Uhud. It is not for us to question God's Plan which is full of wisdom and mercy for all. Our duty is to stand firm and unswerving, to obey, and in steadfast courage, to persevere, to retrieve our mistakes, not in grief and despair, but in firm hope in God and in contempt of pain and death. "(Yusuf Ali, p.154).

Patience is a universal phenomenon and all cultures highly emphasize being patient and understanding. Patience makes a person socially stable, stronger, wiser, and sophisticated person. Men such as Buddha says, "Patience is key. Remember: A jug fills drop by drop". [11]

GRIEF

Before we say a few words about the approaches related to grief in Islamic psychology, we have to define grief according to psychologists. There are two types of grief. "Grief is the psychological emotional experience following a loss of any kind (relationship, status, job, house, game, income, etc.), whereas bereavement is a specific type of grief related to someone dying".[12] In Islamic psychology, grief incurs by external and internal factors. External factors are issues, such as a loss of a loved one, or an enormous mistake that someone has caused, which affects you emotionally. Internal grief, is caused by not controlling our own ego and *nafs;* our own mistakes in life such as a wrong relationship will cause grief. There are many dictum from the Prophet of Islam about grief. The Prophet says, "If you have four things in life you don't need to grieve: honesty in speaking, protecting trust, good manners, and modesty in eating". (Hadith 251, Nahj Al Fasaaha). In another Hadith, "Allah with his wisdom in his blessings has put comfortability and happiness in his will and submission. He put grief and sorrow in suspicion and anger. (Hadith 679, Nahj Al Fasaaha). "Belief in destiny will take away grief and sorrow" (Hadith 1068, Nahj Al, Fasaaha). Islam connects the avoidance of grief to charity in helping others. The Prophet says, "Avoid suffering in grief by giving *sadaqa* (charity) until God removes your suffering" (Hadith 1134, Nahj Al Fasaaha).

According to Islam, grief could sometimes lead to positive outcomes. In some cases, grief leads you to the truth and understanding. The Prophet says, "Get used to sorrow and grief, which is enlightenment of the heart, and keep yourself hungry and thirsty" (Hadith 1971, Nahj Al Fasaaha). Since Muslims believe that destiny is not under their control, they realize that grieving is useless and this is what the Prophet says, "Don't grieve too much what is destined and what is in your sustenance which will reach you" (Hadith 2480, Nahj Al Fasaaha). Islam is a religion of people, the more people reach out to each other, the better society we may have because society is made of people and people should look after each other's goodness. The Prophet says, "Whoever removes the grief of another believer in this world, Allah will remove their grief in the Hereafter" (Hadith 2756, Nahj Al Fasaaha).

Sometimes afflictions, disease, and grief can be the punishment of this world (Hadith 3114, Nahj Al Fasaaha). Muslims believe that whatever we sew, we reap the results. Grief, diseases, and afflictions may have reasons behind them because nothing comes without reasons behind it. We should try our best to avoid internal grief that we cause ourselves because internal grief costs us our long life. The Prophet said that, "Grief is one half of old age" (Hadith 171, Nahj Al Fasaaha).

SUFISM

One of the many things that psychology and Sufism have in common is that they both investigate and analyze the mysteries of the human mind and suggest ways to help the mind improve. In order for us to really understand the concept of Sufism, we first have to know what Sufism really is. "Sufism is the mystical path by, which people seek the truth of Divine, love, and knowledge through direct personal experiences of God" [13]. This mystical path exists in Islam, which is how Sufism is related to Islam. Both Sufism and Islam seek the pleasure of God, His love, and are at peace with themselves and with all other creations such as people, animals, and even nature.

Because one of the main goals of Sufism is to reach God, one has to have knowledge and a clear understanding of the Qur'an and follow the footsteps of the Prophet, step by step, so they may reach the highest level of wisdom, which is what mysticism is. When one attains the highest level of wisdom, they will find the true light of reality and love, which is what makes it a spiritual journey to reach God. A real Sufi does not only practice to clear the mind and the heart for the sake of God; Sufis live for the sake of God alone. Sufis are not after a materialistic lifestyle and their main goal as a Sufi is to please and love their Creator. It is through pure love that one can attain felicity.

As mentioned before, the spirituality and the soul of someone is the way of communication to Allah. There are three principles when it comes to

Sufism: Nafs (self/ego) being the lowest principle; Qalb (heart) which is the second principle, and the first being our Ruh (spirit or soul). Sufis believe that there was a higher soul before our existence that consisted of the Nafs, Qalb, and Ruh, which have the ability to speak to God. This is why it is important to try and keep our best to have our minds, heart, and soul purified, because that is the way for a real communication to Allah. Symbolically, there are four parts of the heart (Qalb) that Sufis derived from the Qur'an, which are Sadr (breast), Fua'd (heart), Lubb (innermost heart), and Qalb (heart). Our Sadr (breasts) are connected with Islam which is mentioned in the Qur'an 39:23. Our Qalb (heart) is the seat of our faith (Qur'an 49:7 and 16:106), fua'd (heart) is connected to the gnosis (Qur'an 53:11), and lastly, the lubb (innermost heart) is the seat of Tawhid (Qur'an 3:190), which is the oneness of God as stated earlier. As Muslims and Sufis, it is very important for us to keep our hearts purified because Allah knows our hearts. The heart, which has to be pure, is one of the most important tools for communication to Him. Without a pure heart, mind, and soul, we are left with a stateless and ignorant mind.

The practice of Sufism not only has mental benefits for us, but also our physical health. "Sufis seek to love according to eternal, selfless, spiritual values, rather than transient, mercenary worldly ones. Neuroscientific studies show that practices like meditations, chanting, and whining all improve harmony between the dualist, verbal, intellect of the brain's left hemisphere and the holistic, silent, poetic, intuition of the right" [14] It's great to know that within the progress of reaching God, there are psychological and biological health benefits that come to it.

DEVELOPMENTAL PSYCHOLOGY

PERSONALITY DEVELOPMENT

Personality refers to an individuals consistent thoughts, emotions, and behaviors in a situation. It is our understanding that family, economic factors, and societal leadership can have an influence on an individual's personality. Especially in contemporary world, the culture of a person can be influenced by economic factors plus the influence of the media that would have an impact on personal behavior and character. The media's impact on citizens has people under the influence of aggressive marketing, gang violence, and political issues. The media propagates the products for their specific consumers and this is how we see the personality traits of individuals in modern industrial capitalist society. People wear specific clothing to show the identity that they want others to perceive. At the same time, the way their communication is designed is a representative not only of their personality but also of their social class.

In Islam, personality develops following the role model of the Prophet Muhammad as noted earlier. Behavior and values are not picked up media or economic factors but only the role model of the Prophet. This is extremely important when one studies an Islamic society. The core principle of a Muslim society in the development of the personalities is *sunnah* (the tradition of living of the Prophet). The Qur'an mentions that the Prophet of Islam is the best example to follow saying,

لَّقَدۡ كَانَ لَكُمۡ فِى رَسُولِ ٱللَّهِ أُسۡوَةٌ حَسَنَةٌ لِّمَن كَانَ يَرۡجُواْ ٱللَّهَ وَٱلۡيَوۡمَ ٱلۡآخِرَ وَذَكَرَ ٱللَّهَ كَثِيرٗا

"You have indeed in the Apostle of God a beautiful pattern (of conduct) for any one whose hope is in God and the Final Day, and who engages much in the praise of God" (Qur'an 33:21).

Muhammad is considered to be the most influential and moral human being in the course of history according to Islamic sources. The Qur'an calls him a blessing to the world. His conduct, manners, attitude, and behavior are noble. In *The 100, A Ranking Of The Most Influential Persons in History* by Michael Hart, the author ranks the Prophet of Islam the number one most influential person in history saying, "My choice of Muhammad to lead the list of the worlds most influential persons may surprise some readers and may be questioned by others, but he was the only man in history who was supremely successful on both the religious and the secular levels". [15]

The difference between Islam and other religions from a socio-psychological point of view is the collection, narrations, and lifestyle of the Prophet Muhammad, which Muslims call *sunnah*. For a Muslim to have a stable pattern of conduct, values, and principles, the *sunnah* is the guideline. The following is what some non-Muslims philosophers and thinkers wrote about Muhammad.

Victor Hugo (1802-1885).

> "O leaders of the believers! As soon as you understood, the world believed in your word. The day in which you were born, a star appeared and three towers in the palace of Khorsu collapsed!" - Victor Hugo (1802-1885).

Napolean Bonaparte as Quotes in Cherfils, 'Bonaparte et Islam'. Paris, France, pp.105, 125.

> "I hope the time is not far off when I shall be able to unite all the wise and educated men of all the countries and establish a uniform regime based on the principles

of Qur'an which alone are true and which alone can lead men to happiness."

Sir George Bernard Shaw in "The Genuine Islam,' Vol. 1, No. 8, 1936

"I have always held the religion of Muhammad in high estimation because of its wonderful vitality. It is the only religion which appears to me to possess that assimilating capacity to the changing phase of existence which can make itself appeal to every age, I have studied him-the wonderful man and in my opinion far from being an anti-Christ, he must be called the Savior of Humanity".

H.G. Wells

"The Islamic teachings have left great traditions for equitable and gentle dealings and behavior, and inspire people with nobility and tolerance. These are human teachings of the highest order and at the same time practicable. These teachings brought into existence a society in which hard-heartedness and collective oppression and injustice were the least as compared with all other societies preceding it...Islam is replete with gentleness, courtesy, and fraternity".

The Qur'an lays great emphasis to follow the guidelines pattern in the tradition of the Prophet. The Qur'an even says that only those will be blessed that follow not only Allah but the footsteps of the Prophet Muhammad saying,

وَأَطِيعُواْ ٱللَّهَ وَٱلرَّسُولَ لَعَلَّكُمْ تُرْحَمُونَ

"Obey God in the Apostle that you may
obtain mercy" (Qur'an 3:132).

In this verse, God placed the obedience of Muhammad alongside with Him and made it in such a command that without following the Prophet footsteps, His mercy will not come to a person.

وَمَن يُطِعِ ٱللَّهَ وَٱلرَّسُولَ فَأُوْلَـٰٓئِكَ مَعَ ٱلَّذِينَ أَنْعَمَ ٱللَّهُ عَلَيْهِم مِّنَ ٱلنَّبِيِّنَ وَٱلصِّدِّيقِينَ وَٱلشُّهَدَآءِ وَٱلصَّـٰلِحِينَۚ وَحَسُنَ أُوْلَـٰٓئِكَ رَفِيقًا

> "Allah says, All who obey God and the Apostle are in the company of those on whom is the Grace of God" (Qur'an 4:69).

And the Qur'an warned people that if they disobey Him and the Prophet, they will bear the consequences. The Qur'an says,

وَأَطِيعُواْ ٱللَّهَ وَأَطِيعُواْ ٱلرَّسُولَ وَٱحْذَرُواْۚ فَإِن تَوَلَّيْتُمْ فَٱعْلَمُوٓاْ أَنَّمَا عَلَىٰ رَسُولِنَا ٱلْبَلَـٰغُ ٱلْمُبِينُ

"Obey God and Obey the Apostle and be aware of evil: if you do turn back know you that it is our Apostle's duty to proclaim the message in the clearest manner" (Qur'an 5:92).

The above verses clearly answer the importance of following Muhammad's footsteps for conducts, manners, and behavior. Dr. Muhammad Fazl-Ur-Rahman Ansari in his book, *The Qur'anic Foundations and the Structure of Muslim Societies*, writes, "The question, therefore, emerges: what does the *sunnah* stand for? We may concisely answer this question by saying that the Holy Prophet's *sunnah* stands for the dynamic manifestations of the ethico-religious dimensions of his personality". [16]

A true Muslim's character, personality, and behavior is shaped by his mentor and role model, the Prophet Muhammad. The interesting point is that psychologically a Muslim strongly believes that following the footsteps of the Prophet Muhammad in this life guarantees him social dignity and integrity as well as secures him a place in paradise. This can be considered the highest level of personality development in a person that he not only thinks of his living life, but also is convinced of life after death.

Without, a moral and ethical role model such as the Prophet, a negative, awkward, and confusing personality may develop out of egoism and selfishness. The concepts of narcissism and psychopath are good examples of negative personalities. Narcissism is defined as follows, "Narcissistic personality disorder is a mental disorder in which people have an inflated sense of their own importance, a deep need for admiration and a lack of empathy for others. But behind this mask of ultra confidence lies a fragile self-esteem that's vulnerable to the slightest criticism". [17] Narcissism develops due to the lack of a proper mentor and role model, and based on this study on personality development, it is extremely important that people be aware especially for who they elect as their leader. Society as a whole would not know how to deal with a narcissist person and a narcissist person would not know how to lead a society. [17]

By the same token, another default of personality is psychopathy. According to the English dictionary, someone with a psychopathic personality will manifest themselves with amoral and antisocial behavior, has the lack of ability to love or establish meaningful personal relationships, has extreme egocentricity, fails to learn from experience, etc. Again, these types of individuals could have the highest education but they would still lack the biological ability for empathy. From a social point of view, a psychopath lacks the moral and ethical mentor to uphold him in society so he could behave normally. The bottom line, is that in personality development, even if there are some biological traits but not a mental disease, people can be trained with love, compassion, care, and support to become a better social being.

When people do not have proper role modeling and mentors, they feel trapped into the arena of some motivational speakers that influence people deeply to the extent that leads to destruction and crime. James Jones and James Arthur Ray are good examples of motivational speakers who became obsessed with their own ego, eventually created a cult and led people to their own death. This is a misery of a society or people whom are influenced by those who are not psychologically fit themselves.

CHILD DEVELOPMENT

Child development in Islam is extremely important because children will be the future of their families and societies. In Islam, the development of a child begins before birth. The Qur'an says,

خَلَقَ ٱلْإِنسَـٰنَ مِنْ عَلَقٍ

"Created man out of Alaq (adhesive living organism)" (Qur'an 96:2).

This verse alludes to the very early stages of creation. It is at this point that several steps and measurements need to be taken. The two steps are kindness and gentleness to the mother and proper nutrition to the mother.

Abdullah Yusuf Ali writes, "The lowly origin of the animal in man is contrasted with the high destiny offered to him in his intellectual, moral, and spiritual nature by his "most bountiful" Creator. No knowledge is withheld from man. On the contrary, through the faculties freely given to him, he acquires it in such measures as outstrip his immediate understanding, leads him to ever strive for newer and newer meaning". (Yusuf Ali, The Qur'an 1761, Commentary 6205). On the same chapter, the Qur'an says,

عَلَّمَ ٱلْإِنسَـٰنَ مَا لَمْ يَعْلَمْ

"Taught man that which he knew not" (Qur'an 96:5).

Human beings are created from a blank slate. The above verse is referring to a blank slate, that mankind does not know anything and the Creator is the one who teaches him while developing as a human being. Yusuf Ali writes, "God teaches us new knowledge at every given moment. Individuals learn more and more, day by day; nations and humanities at large learn fresh knowledge at every stage. This is even more noticeable and important in the spiritual world. (Yusuf Ali, The Qur'an, Commentary 6207).

Developmental psychology, the progressive changes in behavior of an individual over time, has been studied among Muslim scholars for ages. There are two sets of learning in early development: natural and adaptation. The natural learning are those concepts in development that the child acts and reacts naturally such as sucking a nipple of the mother or the rooting reflex, when one places an object in the palm of the infant, which is the grasping reflex. The reflex when somebody calls him or touches the infant is the Moro reflex, is advocated with sudden loss of support, loud noise, or when the infant feels as if it is falling. These actions are natural but are coined by modern psychologists. The adaptation where the environment affects the parenting style, thinking abilities, moral and ethical values are acquired phenomenon that depend upon the upbringing of a child. As we noted earlier, Islam put a great emphasis on knowledge. The Prophet Muhammad said "learning is mandatory for all men and women". This means that educated and literate parents will have success in developing their child. Unfortunately, most parents are illiterate and as a result, not only are the developmental stages weak, but the different developmental stages all the way to full grown maturity are also damaged due to lack of proper training.

PSYCHOLOGY OF AGING

Aging is a natural process. However, the aging process depends upon an individuals' lifestyle, economic strengths and weaknesses, diet, and most importantly the worldview and vision of life as a whole that may contribute to aging and whether it's faster or slower. The Qur'an speaks about natural growth and aging saying,

هُوَ ٱلَّذِى خَلَقَكُم مِّن تُرَابٍ ثُمَّ مِن نُطْفَةٍ ثُمَّ مِنْ عَلَقَةٍ ثُمَّ يُخْرِجُكُمْ طِفْلاً ثُمَّ لِتَبْلُغُوٓاْ أَشُدَّكُمْ ثُمَّ لِتَكُونُوا شُيُوخًا وَمِنكُم مَّن يُتَوَفَّىٰ مِن قَبْلُ وَلِتَبْلُغُوٓاْ أَجَلاً مُّسَمًّى وَلَعَلَّكُمْ تَعْقِلُونَ

"It is He Who has created you from dust then from a sperm-drop, then from a leech-like clot (living adhesive leech like organism); then does he get you out (into the lights) as a child: then lets you (grow and) reach your age of full strength; then lets you become old,-though of you there

49

are some who die before;-and lets you reach a term appointed; in order that you may learn wisdom" (Qur'an 40:67).

This verse clearly is an indication of ontology, which is the process of birth to death. Aging in Islam considered an asset rather than a liability. People are respected because of their experience, wisdom, and the service they render to their families and society.

A person who is God-conscious knows very well, that one day, they will depart this life, and understanding this departure is a fact of life. Everybody knows that living in this world is not eternal. Understanding this fact, psychologically, will give a person of faith the ability to think more deeply about their past life and if the person made any mistakes instead of being remorseful of their mistakes, they are given the opportunity to ask for forgiveness, repent, and even apologize to those whom the person had bad encounters with. This attitude redeems an individual from a lot of stress and negativity, because in the little time they may have ahead, and hope brings them a total satisfaction. This mindset leads them to prayers and supplications, which is good for their weak biological body and at the same time, strengthens their mental ability. What is important, at an old age, is that a God-conscious individual will never feel lonely if they know in their heart that God is with them. They can communicate with Him, ponder, and even at an old age, become energetic and a motivated individual rather than isolated, depressed, and forgotten one. This mindset of positivism can become a role model for their offspring because the offspring does not see a lost and broken physical entity but a wise, understanding, and knowledgeable human being. Study shows that many people in old age become depressed and isolated, and feel useless, which is not the case in Islam. With the power of faith, an old individual can still be a role model of guidance and wisdom for the people surrounding them.

I have been honored to work with a group of senior women, most of whom live by themselves. These women are a source of wisdom simply because they rely on their faith as a guiding principle of their life in old age. Even at the age of 75, these women have goals and objectives spiritually. I was told that they read the Qur'an daily, do not want to miss any days prayers, and constantly pray for their children for their well-being and felicity. They feel independent and believe that no one should rely on their children but on God alone. This mindset, psychologically, keeps them healthy and gives them sense of protection.

Of course, physically, these ladies are naturally afraid, because of their fragility but are not afraid of any sort of illness that is not in their control. Again, as much as they take care for themselves, they also rely on God, even for their fragility. Study shows that one-third of elderly fall without consciously knowing that they're falling. However, a Muslim mindset is a such that they know that they are falling because of reality but at the same time they know that if they are praying, that will give them a sense of security. They consciously know that they are falling, but at the same time, they are also conscious of God's protection, which gives them a strength of mental ability. This does not mean that they are not falling; it means that despise the fact that they know they're falling, their mindset is seeking spiritual guidance to not fall, and psychologically this is important. These women know that but still they ask God to protect them that this should not happen to them. Psychologically, that is a reliability on the power of self.

BIO-PSYCHOLOGY

BIOLOGICAL PSYCHOLOGY

The Qur'an was revealed as a complete guidance to mankind. This guidance is not only a set of moral and ethical rules but contains legal, political, social, and scientific principles. The Qur'an says,

ٱلْيَوْمَ أَكْمَلْتُ لَكُمْ دِينَكُمْ وَأَتْمَمْتُ عَلَيْكُمْ نِعْمَتِى وَرَضِيتُ لَكُمُ ٱلْإِسْلَـٰمَ دِينًا

فَمَنِ ٱضْطُرَّ فِى مَخْمَصَةٍ غَيْرَ مُتَجَانِفٍ لِّإِثْمٍ فَإِنَّ ٱللَّهَ غَفُورٌ رَّحِيمٌ

"This day I have perfected for you your religion and completed My favor upon you and have approved for you Islam as your religion. But whoever is forced by severe hunger with no inclination to sin-then indeed, Allah is Forgiving and Merciful" (Qur'an 5:3).

The above verse indicates that Allah has given the most perfect and complete book of guidance to mankind and chosen Islam as their religion. Two points need to be elaborated in this verse:

A: Islam, in this context, has a scientific meaning and that is asking mankind to accept the law of nature as Allah's creation, where mankind is included in this creation. This means that, allegorically law of nature and law of Allah are one and the same as noted earlier. This is a total Tawhid and this is what Islam is all about. Oneness of Allah and His creation.

B: Religion, the actual Arabic word is "Deen" that has been translated as religion. As a matter of fact, *Deen* means more than just religion; *Deen*

55

is a complete way of life as indicated in the verse. There is no equivalent word for Deen in Latin or in the English literature. The word religion comes from *religio,* which is derived from *relegere*, which means to do something over and over again without questioning or pondering.

Ibn Sina (Avicenna 980-1037), a Muslim physician, philosopher, mathematician, astronomer, for the first time, mentioned in his books of Al'Shifa, the relationship between psychological functioning emphasizing cognition with biological entities and emphasizing the brain. Without question, he was the first physician who brought up the issue of biological entities.

According to Islam, mankind is made of corpse and spirit. Aristotle, the Greek philosopher (384 BC-322 BC), called mankind hylo-morphic. According to the Qur'an, Allah has given His spirit to mankind and this is what the Qur'an says, "When I have fashioned him in due proportion and breathed into him of My spirit, fall you down in obeisance unto him" (Qur'an 15:29). However, Allah asked mankind to not question His spirit. This is the verse of the Qur'an that says,

وَيَسْـَٔلُونَكَ عَنِ ٱلرُّوحِ ۖ قُلِ ٱلرُّوحُ مِنْ أَمْرِ رَبِّى وَمَآ أُوتِيتُم مِّنَ ٱلْعِلْمِ إِلَّا قَلِيلًا

"They ask thee concerning the Spirit (of inspiration). Say: "The Spirit (cometh) by command of my Lord: of knowledge it is only a little that is communicated to you, (O men!)" (Qur'an 17:85).

So far, and it will never happen, no one truly understands the nature of the Holy Spirit. Is it the mind? Is it the soul? Is it the non-physical heart? There is no proof. Because Allah's spirit being in mankind, He is always with mankind and this is what He says in the Qur'an,

وَلَقَدْ خَلَقْنَا ٱلْإِنسَـٰنَ وَنَعْلَمُ مَا تُوَسْوِسُ بِهِۦ نَفْسُهُۥ ۖ وَنَحْنُ أَقْرَبُ إِلَيْهِ مِنْ حَبْلِ ٱلْوَرِيدِ

"It was We Who created Man, and We know what dark suggestions his souls makes to him: for We are nearer to him than (his) jugular vein." (Qur'an 50:16).

MALE AND FEMALE BRAIN

The study of the brain is vital for two main reasons: first it is the brain that we use to study the mind. Secondly, study of the brain reveals that men and women are created equal from intelligence point of view. Allah has given mankind the human brain to make the best of all His Creations and to differentiate us from other species. He has given us the best ability to think, understand, analyze, decision-making, to love and to learn. As a human race, we have used our gifted abilities to advance more and more throughout centuries such as advancing in technology, medicine, and just as a human race in general. These abilities are how we have come to be who we are as a mankind today.

He has given males and females equal mental abilities; unfortunately, there is the belief that males are more intelligent, that they have some mental abilities that females lack or that females acquire some abilities that males lack. There is the belief that an individual either has a male or a female brain. For many years, as our technology and discoveries in science advance, researchers have been trying to find evidence by looking at brain scans and trying to find similarities and differences between the male and female brain. A recent study led by Daphna Joel at Tel Aviv University, who researched the sex differences across the human race, showed that there is no such thing as a male or female brain. The study revealed that an individual's brain rarely has all 'male' traits or all 'female' traits instead it's more like a mixed bag-some things are more common in women, some things more common in men, and some are common in both. [18]

Like stated before, there is an idea that people either have a "male" or a "female" brain. Joel says, "The theory goes that once a fetus develops testicles, they secrete testosterone which masculinizes the brain, if that were true, there would be two types of brains". To test this theory out, Joel and her colleagues looked for similarities and differences from 1400 brain scans from people aged 13 to 85. They also searched for variations in the size and connections between the brain regions. According to their findings, sex differences in brain structure do exist, but an individuals' brain is likely to be just that "individual, with a mix of features. [19]

Allah has not given males or females different or more mental abilities. He has not made one gender smarter than the other, or more capable of doing things than one another. We are all born with full mental abilities but it is up to us to use the most of what He has provided for us. However, the Qur'an says,

وَلِلرِّجَالِ عَلَيْهِنَّ دَرَجَةٌ

"Men have a degree above women" (Qur'an 2:228).

We understand that there is no difference between the male and female brain from a scientific point of view. The Qur'an raises the question that men are a "degree" above women. When we studied the male brain and the female brain, we also found out that the male brain is slightly larger than of female's. The term "daraja" (degree) is a mathematical concept, not an economic one that most scholars in the past have interpreted. "Degree" is a physical and physiological aspect of creation that men are physically created more stronger than females, but this does not mean that female are weaker intellectually, spiritually, and mentally. This is very clear from verse one of the fourth chapter of the Qur'an saying:

يَـٰٓأَيُّهَا ٱلنَّاسُ ٱتَّقُواْ رَبَّكُمُ ٱلَّذِى خَلَقَكُم مِّن نَّفْسٍ وَٰحِدَةٍ

"O mankind! Reverence your Guardian Lord
who created you from a single soul"
(Qur'an 4:1).

As we mentioned earlier, mankind being male or female are created from the same sperm, leech-like adhesive matter and both are created from the Earth. All this tells us that there is no difference of male and female from a creation point of view, except that men are a "degree" higher because of their physical strength. This is the law of physics that we have to have positive and negative in order to compliment a phenomenon such as this one. Let's give a very simple example and that is the battery of a car. It has a plus and a minus pole. If the battery has two pluses, it will not spark. By the same token, if it has two minuses, it will not spark. It must be a positive and a negative pole to spark and make things happen. This way men and women also complement each other one being less "physically" strong and one being "physically" stronger. Laws of physics apply in creation. If we accept the previous explanation that men are a "degree" above because they are the provider, this cannot be justified for a women who is not married. Even if a woman who has a father, a brother, and a husband; it is up to the woman to be able to provide for herself. There is the old belief that still carries on today in traditional cultures that a man is to have the role to provide for the women and that women cannot be providers, but what if there is no man to provide for women? It is up to women themselves to be just as independent instead of sufficient.

HEALTH AND STRESS MANAGEMENT

According to the Qur'an, mankind has been created to worship Him. The Qur'an says,"

وَمَا خَلَقْتُ ٱلْجِنَّ وَٱلْإِنسَ إِلَّا لِيَعْبُدُونِ

I have only created Jinn and men, that they
may serve Me" (Qur'an 51:56).

It is important to worship Allah with good health and well-being, because no one can worship Him properly, unless they're in a good state of mind and health. The definition of worship in Islam is not just praying or meditation; worship means all aspects of life that benefit the individual and society such as being respectful to parents, helping the poor, studying, being kind to neighbors, even when one greets someone whom he does not know him; that's an act of worship. In other words, anything that Allah recommends or there is a maxim of the Prophet that is followed by the believer, he is in the state of worship.

Imaam Al Ghazali (Died 505 of Lunar Calendar) mentioned in his most popular book, *Alchemy of Happiness,* that the reason we eat food is to get energy to worship Allah. Psychologically and physically, there are two aspects of well-being. One, by eating properly to energize the whole body and two, is for the spiritual well-being that flourishes by prayers, supplications, and the remembrance of God.

Nutrition- There are important elements in nutrition for psychological well-being.

Lawful Income: This is the source of a Muslim psychological well-being. If a Muslim is stealing, robbing, or drug dealing, then they are earning unlawful income and the sustenance earned is not lawful, their food is not lawful, and consequently, their well-being isn't either. Unlawful income breeds unlawful acts of wrongdoing. The state of mind is always at peace when one makes honest money for living.

Clean Food: Food must be clean to avoid any source of disease. However, food should also be natural. In Islam, mankind is a natural entity and must consume natural food. If food is unnatural and contains many added chemicals, this will pollute the body. Unnatural elements in the body in the long run will cause unknown damage that is hard to detect. Nutrition is part of a good health and well-being. Sometimes, natural and healthy food may not be delicious because of its organic nature, but it is good for the body. By the same token, some elements of nutrition may be delicious but could also be harmful for the body. That is why in Islam, as well as Judaism, there are specific laws regarding diet to protect the body and mind from harmful elements.

Eating Less: Eating less is beneficial for our health. Studies have shown that a reduction in calories could be associated with a longer life. Research shows that when mice are given less food, the reduction in calories slows down a number of genetic aging processes. A study was conducted that people could benefit from calorie reduction; after two years of conducting the research, participants reported significantly better psychological effects, in comparison to another group of participants who ate whatever they wanted. The group having to reduce their calories reported having an improved mood, reduced tension, general health, and even weight loss. A research was conducted in 2014 from the NYU Langome Medical Centre; "when fed 30 percent fewer calories, female mice showed less activity in almost 900 different genes linked to aging processes in the brain, suggesting that eating less might slow down the cognitive decline that comes with age". [20] The bottom line is that whatever people consume, the food will have a direct impact on their mind and health. As the saying goes, you are what you eat. Fourteen hundred years ago the Prophet of Islam suggested that people should eat less and they should stop eating before they are satiated. There is another meaningful hadith of the Prophet, which says: stomach is the depot of all diseases.

1. **Nature:** Like us, food has nature. For example, walnut are considered to be a warm food, which is good to be consumed during winter, and cucumbers are considered to be a cold food, which is good to be considered during summer. According to Islamic psychology of dietary system, one has to know their nature before consuming food. There are kids who are allergic to peanuts. This does not mean that peanuts are generally harmful to everyone; it simply means that peanuts do not fit the biological nature of those allergic to it. Humans are part of the natural system and their nature must be aligned with the natural laws.

2. **Fasting:** Psychologically, the body needs to rest and to be cleaned from harmful elements that are deposited into our system. "Fasting is a socio-psychological concept for our well-being. Fasting has been found to be an effective treatment for psychological and emotional disorders. It helps a person to firm up their will, cultivate, refine their taste, manners, strengthen their convictions of doing good, avoid controversy, petulance and rashness, which all contribute towards a sane and healthy personality. Besides nurturing resistance, the ability to face hardships and endurance, fasting reflects on outward physical appearance by cutting out gluttony and getting rid of excess fat. The benefits of fasting on health do not stop there but are instrumental in alleviating a number of physical diseases, including those of the digestive systems, such as chronic stomachache, inflammation of the colon, liver diseases, indigestion, and conditions such as obesity, arteriosclerosis, high blood pressure, asthma, diphtheria and many other maladies." [21]

SPIRITUAL WELL-BEING:

According to Islam, humans are spiritual beings and spirituality distinguishes the biological aspects of humans from animals. Spirituality within the human mind is gifted from the Creator saying,

وَيَسْـَٔلُونَكَ عَنِ ٱلرُّوحِ قُلِ ٱلرُّوحُ مِنْ أَمْرِ رَبِّى وَمَآ أُوتِيتُم مِّنَ ٱلْعِلْمِ إِلَّا قَلِيلًا

"The Spirit is one of the commands of my Lord. You have only been given a little knowledge" (Qur'an 17:85).

According to Islamic psychology, mankind has the spirit of God with them based on the above verse. So this spirit is not only a gift from God to mankind, but it is the source of all energy that makes us human. Mankind has never been alone and God has, and forever will, be with them. As He says,

وَلَقَدْ خَلَقْنَا ٱلْإِنسَٰنَ وَنَعْلَمُ مَا تُوَسْوِسُ بِهِ نَفْسُهُ ۖ وَنَحْنُ أَقْرَبُ إِلَيْهِ مِنْ حَبْلِ ٱلْوَرِيدِ

"And We have already created man and know what his soul whispers to him, and We are closer to him than [his] jugular vein" (Qur'an 50:16).

The spirit of Allah within the human mind is not only the source of energy but a vital force of action. However, the happiness of this spirit is in the human hands. The only way that the spirit within us could be happy is when we submit, perform prayers, and trust Allah's mercy on us. Allah constantly asks humans to pray for Him five times daily. The question is this: Does He need our prayers or do we need to pray for our own happiness? The answer is that Allah is not in need of our prayers, it is humans that need to pray for Him to elevate our sources of energy. The spirit within us will be motivated, sparked, and energized when regular prayers are performed. Lack of prayers in daily life makes people less motivated spiritually and consequently, they become materialistic. Lack of spirituality causes stress, depression, fatigue, loss of hope, and hatred. This is because humans, as a spiritual being, do not have anything to rely upon but their own strength, and when this strength is weakened, the only thing that can gain support is total submission to the Creator. Spirituality grants a person total satisfaction of the heart, mind, and gets them out of confusion and illusion. People lacking spirituality go astray and damage themselves resorting to drugs, immoral acts, etc. The human body needs nurturing and this nurturing is both physical and spiritual; they go along together. If the nurturing of our body stops, the body will malfunction and if the nurturing of our spirituality stops, the mind will stop functioning properly. As Aristotle said, humans are hylo-morphic being made of spirit and body.

Anger is a natural and an emotional process. Anger is different in others and depends upon people's upbringing, knowledge of the art of living, background, profession and even diet. If one is in a domestic violent atmosphere, the result is a negative attitude or if brought up with a spoiling approach then the result is being aggressive, demanding, or very stubborn. When one is brought up in a discriminatory atmosphere such as men seeing themselves above women at home, the result is negative attitude towards women; this is wrong because Islam teaches us equality. Most of the time, parents fail to teach their children the art of living like teaching them how to be respectful to others, how to be logical on different issues, that to be stubborn is not a good quality of life, patience, forgiveness, tolerance or the art of reasoning not suspicion. With good education, teaching the art of living and teaching wisdom can be subdued, because behavior can be changed by proper education. Omar Farouq (May Allah be please with him) was a stubborn person, but after accepting Islam and the role modeling he received from the Prophet, he changed. Sometimes people are working in a negative environment. This happens when people lose the objectivity of life. Diet is another issue that may cause bad temper. Human being is a natural entity according to Islam. If one eats something that is not recommended by the Creator, it will cause negative results. For example Allah explicitly mentions what people should eat or not to eat. This is because He knows what we need for our growth and need. If people violate this principle, this may cause negative attitude. Allah created everything for our moderate use, and if we eat too much or too little that will cause disruption of balance in our system and affect our temper.

Halal meat, vegetables, wheat, rice all are made for our moderate use. The body needs all this based on the climate we live in and the biology that makes up our own nature. Bad tempers could be the result of a variety of issues, but when we claim to be a Muslim, then we have to tackle the problem by Islamic principles. One major task in Islamic psychology is patience and practicing patience. It is not easy for an ordinary person but if a Muslim resorts to the Qur'an and the role model of Prophet Muhammad, then the mercy of Allah is bestowed upon us.

Anger management is learning how to control our anger, which is a very normal emotional state of mind. Not only should we learn how to control it, but learn to forgive others in order to bring peace with them and to ourselves. Ignoring people and cutting relationships with relatives, is not an Islamic principle and is against mode of ethics and morality.

There are varieties of reasons that people get angry according to the socio-psychology of Islam. The Qur'an clearly says,

ٱلَّذِينَ يُنفِقُونَ فِى ٱلسَّرَّآءِ وَٱلضَّرَّآءِ وَٱلْكَـٰظِمِينَ ٱلْغَيْظَ
وَٱلْعَافِينَ عَنِ ٱلنَّاسِ وَٱللَّهُ يُحِبُّ ٱلْمُحْسِنِينَ

"Who suppress their rage, and who pardon people for God loves those who excel in doing good" (Qur'an, 3:134).

Also, the Qur'an says,

فَبِمَا رَحْمَةٍ مِّنَ ٱللَّهِ لِنتَ لَهُمْ وَلَوْ كُنتَ فَظًّا غَلِيظَ ٱلْقَلْبِ لَٱنفَضُّوا مِنْ حَوْلِكَ فَٱعْفُ عَنْهُمْ وَٱسْتَغْفِرْ لَهُمْ وَشَاوِرْهُمْ فِى
ٱلْأَمْرِ فَإِذَا عَزَمْتَ فَتَوَكَّلْ عَلَى ٱللَّهِ إِنَّ ٱللَّهَ يُحِبُّ ٱلْمُتَوَكِّلِينَ

"For had you been harsh and hard-hearted, then they would have disbanded from around you. So pardon them. And ask forgiveness for them. And take counsel with them." (Qur'an, 3:159).

There are a few points that the above two verses address. These verses ask people to not get angry, to forgive people, that if one is harsh to people then people would disperse from them. It is better to confront them, investigate, and resolve the issue rather than to be angry or keep a grudge in the heart. It is always good to communicate anger positively. A the same time, Allah does not love those who are not humble saying,

إِنَّ ٱللَّهَ لا يُحِبُّ مَن كَانَ مُخْتَالاً فَخُورًا

"Indeed, God does not love anyone who is self-conceited, boastful" (Qur'an, 4:36).

Also, Allah forbids people to be aggressive by saying,

إِنَّ ٱللَّهَ لا يُحِبُّ ٱلْمُعْتَدِينَ

"Indeed, God does not love the transgressors" (Qur'an, 5:87).

We can clearly see that Allah condemns anger, aggression, selfishness, and loves those who act against these evil emotions. In our Islamic family and community, there are few things that make people angry:

When people's rights are violated. For example, freedom of mind is a God given right, and if someone violates this right and prohibits you from saying what you like to say in this case, a family gathering should take place and very respectfully the issue should be discussed. Or if families get angry at each other over inheritance issues, this should be discussed amicably. If this does not help, then some elders outside the family should be consulted. If this step fails, then a person should resort to the court of law and seek a judge's advice. People's rights could be violated at home or society.

People get angry when they hear something about themselves behind their back, which is a gossip. Someone reports something they hear to another person. This act of reporting is "Haram" (Prohibited) because it is considered a gossip. Gossiping, backbiting, spying and suspicion are all haram in Islam. Whatever Allah has made haram and we do, otherwise, is a great sin. The Qur'an says,

يَٰأَيُّهَا ٱلَّذِينَ ءَامَنُوا ٱجْتَنِبُوا كَثِيرًا مِّنَ ٱلظَّنِّ إِنَّ بَعْضَ ٱلظَّنِّ إِثْمٌ وَلَا تَجَسَّسُوا وَلَا يَغْتَب بَّعْضُكُم بَعْضًا

"O you who believe! Shun much suspicion. For, indeed, certain kinds of suspicion are sinful. Nor should you spy on each other. Nor shall you backbite one another." (Qur'an, 49:12)

According to the Qur'an backbiting and gossiping is like eating a brother's flesh, and the above verse continues saying,

أَيُحِبُّ أَحَدُكُمْ أَن يَأْكُلَ لَحْمَ أَخِيهِ مَيْتًا فَكَرِهْتُمُوهُ ۚ وَٱتَّقُواْ ٱللَّهَ ۚ إِنَّ ٱللَّهَ تَوَّابٌ رَّحِيمٌ

"Would any of you like to eat his dead brother's flesh? You would, most surely, abhor it. So fear God. Indeed, God is all-relenting, mercy-giving." (Qur'an, 49: 12).

It is against Islamic morality that one accepts anything when reported to him that causes animosity. The person should contact that person and consult with him instead of being angry. The irony is that most of the time the closest person in people's lives can fabricate things, lie, and create an atmosphere of hate and animosity and the victim accepts it. Therefore, suspicion is a sin and should be avoided. The solution for this is that we should not accept anything unless we hear it or see it ourselves. If someone else reports to us that which gives us a bad feeling about that person, we should know, even if he or she is the closest person to us that he or she violated Allah's law and committed wrongdoing by gossiping. We should always report to each other good news not bad news that may cause problems between family members or friends.

People get angry because they are oppressed for economic reasons, social reasons, labor exploitation and the like. No one should allow being exploited and should stand firm for his/her rights. The Qur'an condemns oppression saying,

وَٱللَّهُ لَا يُحِبُّ ٱلظَّالِمِينَ

"For God does not love the oppressors." (Qur'an, 3:140), or

وَٱللَّهُ لَا يَهْدِى ٱلْقَوْمَ ٱلظَّالِمِينَ

"For God does not guide the oppressors." (Qur'an, 2: 258).

In the history of the United States many fought against oppression but three African Americans, two men and one woman, who stood high in their struggle were Martin Luther King, Malcolm X, and Rosa Parks (May they all be at peace). No one should be allowed to be oppressed or oppress others. Oppression of any kind including husband to wife, such as spousal abuse, is against human dignity and integrity.

Accusation is another form of immoral approach that makes people angry. In this case, the accused should ask for solid proof. If there is no constructive proof, three witnesses whom are not related, should witness the wrongdoing. One person who is related to the accuser is not solid proof because that person could be biased and would be fabricated between the accuser and his/her associate or friend. In case of adultery, the Qur'an asks people to bring forward four witnesses. Nowadays, when people fail to achieve their evil desires, they resort to accusation. This is very much true with celebrities and people of fame. This also may have been caused by jealousy, and the Qur'an condemns jealousy, asking people to pray that they are safe from an evil-eye saying,

$$وَمِن شَرِّ حَاسِدٍ إِذَا حَسَدَ$$

And from the mischief of the envious one as he practices envy (Qur'an 113:5)

People get angry when they hear some viewpoints that are different than their own. This includes religious matters. Human being are created free and have freedom to think. If your view is different from others, that is because you are human being and not a sheep. The Qu'an says,

$$إِنَّكُمْ لَفِى قَوْلٍ مُخْتَلِفٍ$$

Surely you are of varying opinion (Qur'an 51:8)

And the Prophet said, "The difference of opinion is a blessing of my ummah." We should all learn how to accept each other's viewpoints without getting angry. We do not need to accept what one says but should respect it.

Families have high expectations from each other. We should lower our expectations even from our children and preserve our independence. Many people get angry because their surrounding does not meet their expectation. We should accept others without undue expectations.

People get angry when someone borrows money from them and he does not return it on time. Lending money should be in the form of writing in the presence of two witnesses according to the Qur'an. The letter should be notarized. If we fail to do so, we better take the consequences and be angry with ourselves that we violated the Quranic principles.

Another area that makes people angry is to interfere in someone's life. In our community, this happens often that family members interfere in each other's business. The reason people interfere in our life is because we allow them to do so. It is our own weaknesses, when someone interferes in our life. We should politely and firmly convey the message to not interfere unless asked for advice. In this regard the Qur'an says,

وَلَا تَجَسَّسُواْ

And spy not or interfere (Qur'an 49:12)

The Prophet said: The most distinguished people are those who do not interfere in people's affairs. We should all remember that no one is perfect. We all make mistakes. If we make a mistake, then we better apologize. And people should forgive. But if one makes a mistake and does not apologize, then they are selfish. Pious people are those who apologize and who forgive.

The Prophet recommends when someone is angry, they should perform wudu (ablution). This way, one cools off his anger. Also, the Prophet recommended that one better lie down to cool anger.

Humans are made of qualities that are positive and negative energies that put their *nafs* (soul) into a huge challenge. A Muslim should use and promote their positive energy rather than negative energy into action and practice. This can happen if we use the most sophisticated gifts that Allah has given to us, which is *Aql* (intelligence), and think positively.

Another issue that makes people angry, is we expect people including our family members, to think like us, dress like us, behave like us, and see the world like we do. This is impossible and against human nature. In regard of manners, if family members have learned some manners before the age of 18, that will continue in their adulthood. If they have not learned social manners and they don't try to learn, it is better to accept them the way they are. If Muslims deliberately stay away from the source of knowledge, that is the Qur'an, and the tradition of the Prophet, that is a bad choice they made, and we cannot force them. This problem is rooted in people's childhood where they were not taught proper civic education. One of the major problems that parents do not pay attention to is to teach their children listening skills. And if a person in adulthood behaves uncivilly—not respecting people's opinion, disrespecting elders, being stubborn, not knowing his/her position within family circles or society, this all relates to lack of civic education. This can be learned since civic education is acquired knowledge. If people after the age of 18, do not listen, that is their problem. These people will have a problem with themselves as well as with others. Better ignore them rather than argue with them because they have not learned reasoning.

Some people, including family members, lose the side of humility and they think they are better than others. This sense of superiority not only isolates them but also make people think negative about them. Islam teaches humility and God only acknowledges people on the basis of piety.

The Qur'an teaches us patience. In all aspects of life, a Muslim should practice patience. Patience is a virtue. Cutting relationships with fellow Muslims in the family or outside is not Islamic. Islam teaches brotherhood, compassion and cooperation. It is obvious that we cannot love everyone including our family members, but Islam teaches us to respect each other. That is why Muslim families should base their relationship on Islamic values, Allah showers us with love and people should love each other. The main reason that we have problems in our communities or families, is because the obedience of Allah does not exist and the love for the Prophet has disappeared. Islam, as a civilized way of life, only works for us if we put it into action in our daily lives.

HUMAN SEXUALITY

Human sexuality as perceived in Islam is part of the natural system of reproduction and psychological satisfaction. Islam sees the relationship between men and women as a natural and most important aspect of a family. According to the Qur'an, men and women are created to bestow comfort and bring tranquility of mind to each other. The Qur'an says,

يَـٰٓأَيُّهَا ٱلنَّاسُ ٱتَّقُوا۟ رَبَّكُمُ ٱلَّذِى خَلَقَكُم مِّن نَّفْسٍ وَٰحِدَةٍ وَخَلَقَ مِنْهَا زَوْجَهَا وَبَثَّ مِنْهُمَا رِجَالاً كَثِيرًا وَنِسَآءً ۚ وَٱتَّقُوا۟ ٱللَّهَ

ٱلَّذِى تَسَآءَلُونَ بِهِۦ وَٱلْأَرْحَامَ ۚ إِنَّ ٱللَّهَ كَانَ عَلَيْكُمْ رَقِيبًا (١)

"O mankind! Reverence your guardian Lord who Created you from a single soul, Created, of like nature, his mate, and from them twin scattered (like seeds) countless men and women. Mind Allah through whom you demand your mutual rights and reverence the wombs that bore you for Allah is ever a watcher over you" (Qur'an 4:1)

And,

وَمِنْ ءَايَـٰتِهِۦٓ أَنْ خَلَقَ لَكُم مِّنْ أَنفُسِكُمْ أَزْوَٰجًا لِّتَسْكُنُوٓا۟ إِلَيْهَا وَجَعَلَ بَيْنَكُم مَّوَدَّةً وَرَحْمَةً ۚ
إِنَّ فِى ذَٰلِكَ لَءَايَـٰتٍ لِّقَوْمٍ يَتَفَكَّرُونَ

"In among His signs is this, that He Created for you mates from among yourselves, that you may dwell in tranquility with them, and He has put love and mercy between your hearts, verily in that are sign for those who reflect" (Qur'an 30:21)

The above two verses clearly indicate that men and women are created for each other as natural entities to complement and dwell in tranquility. According to Islamic psychology, men and women are supports and partners for each other. The Qur'an says,

هُنَّ لِبَاسٌ لَّكُمْ وَأَنتُمْ لِبَاسٌ لَّهُنَّ

"Women are clothing for men and men are clothing for women" (Qur'an 2:187).

This means men and women morally support each other and comfort each other psychologically and protect each other's dignity and integrity. Based on the above verse, men and women are completed as a pair. According to Islam, no woman will be complete without a man and no man will be complete without a woman; recognizing in and acknowledging their existence as human beings. In other words, the association of the two makes them realize about their own physical, biological, and psychological being.

Sexual relation is an important aspect of human life, "Muslims of early centuries believed that sexual deprivation could lead to mental and physical disturbances bordering on insanity. One observer related that a group of people had decided to abstain for ascetic reasons, but soon they developed physical as well as mental abnormalities, especially depression and fatigue. It was wildly believed that sexual deprivation was contrary to the preservation of the human species, harmful to health, and destructive of moral integrity".[22] Having said this, human relations are not only for reproduction but also a necessity for psychological well-being. That is an objective between the two sexes. Maulanah Abdul A'Ala Maudoodi wrote about love and compassion between two sexes, "Love and compassion not only enables the spouses to lead a happy and peaceful family life, but also gives them the strength needed for the promotion of higher cultural values" [23]

Since *nikah* (wedlock) is a contract between a man and a woman, their sexual relations are also based on equality. "The Holy Qur'an in various places proclaims the equality of men and women on almost every plane moral, spiritual, and intellectual. By a single masterly stroke, Islam removed the stigma of "wickedness" and "impurity" which the religions of the world had placed upon women. Man and woman, it proclaimed, had both come from the same essence, and, therefore, if woman could be said to be wicked, man also should be regarded as such, or if man had a single sparks of nobility in him, women also should have it. "Women", declare the Holy Prophet Muhammad "Are the twin-halves of men" [24]

Reproduction is a natural process in our creation. The Qur'an uses the term of pair as *zauj* for human reproduction. Human beings are a natural entity and are part of the natural system. By natural law, just like the animal kingdom, human beings are required to be a pair. Professor Bucaille writes, "One of a pair is the translation of *zauj* (plural *azwaj)* whose original meaning is:' that which, in the company of another, forms a pair'; the world is used just as readily for a married couple as for a pair of shoes".[25] This means that the primary association of a man and a woman in Islam is reproduction that eventually establishes a family in which sociologically is the first unit of a Muslim society.

Sexual interaction and intercourse is a natural phenomenon in the Qur'an which says,

نِسَآؤُكُمْ حَرْثٌ لَّكُمْ فَأْتُواْ حَرْثَكُمْ أَنَّىٰ شِئْتُمْ

وَقَدِّمُواْ لِأَنفُسِكُمْ وَٱتَّقُواْ ٱللَّهَ وَٱعْلَمُوٓاْ أَنَّكُم مُّلَـٰقُوهُ وَبَشِّرِ ٱلْمُؤْمِنِينَ

"Your wives are as a tilth unto you; so approach your tilth when or how ye will; but do some good act for your souls beforehand; and fear God and know that ye are to meet Him (in the Hereafter), and give (these) good tidings to those who believe" (Qur'an 2:223).

The above verse explains that the Qur'an sees sexual intercourse as natural acts for human beings for reproduction. It requires that a man should behave appropriately when it comes to sexual intercourse. This is the psychological aspect of sexuality. He should make his partner ready for intercourse so the conception can be a very pleasant and comfortable. At the end of the verse, God asks men and women to be of conscious that any wrongdoing will damage their status in the Hereafter, alluding that mankind will meet their Creator. This is important because intercourse, in human perspective, is not an animalistic mode of behavior but a well mannered approach that includes dignity and respect for the partner. God connects this matter with a conscience-oriented mindset for those who believe. The overall understanding of the verse psychologically is that any approach on sexual matter without peace, harmony, and a pleasant atmosphere are considered to be animalistic behavior, which is not acceptable in Islam.

HOMOSEXUALITY

The main reason that homosexuality is prohibited in Islam is because it is against the natural law of human reproduction and is a source of different diseases that people can develop such as AIDS and HIV. "As the world's leading AIDS researchers gather for the International AIDS Conference in Washington, D.C., scientists report that despite gains in controlling the spread of HIV, the disease has continued to spread at an alarming rate in the very population in which it first appeared — gay men. In a series of papers in the Lancet dedicated to the dynamics of HIV among gay men — a group epidemiologists define as men who have sex with men (MSM) — scientists say that the continued burden of AIDS in this group is due to a combination of lifestyle and biological factors that put these men at higher risk. Rates are rising in all countries around the world." [26]

Knowing all of this, the Qur'an says,

وَلُوطًا إِذْ قَالَ لِقَوْمِهِ أَتَأْتُونَ ٱلْفَاحِشَةَ مَا سَبَقَكُم بِهَا مِنْ أَحَدٍ مِّنَ ٱلْعَٰلَمِينَ (٨٠) إِنَّكُمْ لَتَأْتُونَ ٱلرِّجَالَ شَهْوَةً مِّن دُونِ

ٱلنِّسَاءِ ۚ بَلْ أَنتُمْ قَوْمٌ مُّسْرِفُونَ (٨١) وَمَا كَانَ جَوَابَ قَوْمِهِ إِلَّا أَن قَالُوٓا أَخْرِجُوهُم مِّن قَرْيَتِكُمْ ۖ إِنَّهُمْ أُنَاسٌ

يَتَطَهَّرُونَ (٨٢) فَأَنجَيْنَٰهُ وَأَهْلَهُ إِلَّا ٱمْرَأَتَهُ كَانَتْ مِنَ ٱلْغَٰبِرِينَ (٨٣) وَأَمْطَرْنَا عَلَيْهِم مَّطَرًا ۖ فَٱنظُرْ كَيْفَ كَانَ

عَٰقِبَةُ ٱلْمُجْرِمِينَ (٨٤)

"We also (sent) Lut: He said to his people: "Do ye commit lewdness such as no people in creation (ever) committed before you? For ye practice your lusts on men in preference to women: ye are indeed a people transgressing beyond bounds." And his people gave no answer but this: They said, "Drive them out of your city: these are indeed men who want to be clean and pure!" But we saved him and his family, except his wife: she was of those who lagged behind and we rained down on them a shower (of brimstone): then see what was the end of those who indulged in sin and crime!" (Qur'an 7:80-84).

COGNITIVE PSYCHOLOGY

COGNITION

Cognitive Psychology is the study of the mind and all mental processes, including learning, memory, attention, perception, reasoning, language, conceptual development, and decision-making. In this area, Islamic psychology emphasizes reading, thinking, observing, learning, and traveling. These are the major principles of cognitive development in Islamic psychology. The first revelation to humanity by the Qur'an was "to read". This very short but powerful word from Allah to Muhammad was not intended that he should read only the revealed scripture but it was a vast meaning emphasizing knowledge for humanity that no one can prosper in this life without proper knowledge and education. Later the Prophet said, "The first thing God created was the pen". These two dictums, one from God and one from the Prophet, laid the foundation of Islamic civilization, that is to read and to write with the pen. Reading expands the mind; it leads to exploration, creativity, and conceptualization of the world. The more one reads, starting with the Qur'an, the more he/she expands his/her horizon for learning.

READING

Reading or the intention for reading is to learn the subject matter. Reading and learning together prepare the mind for more exploration and ideas for development, which is why the Qur'an says "O my lord! Advance me in knowledge" (Qur'an, 20:114). Based upon this verse, the Prophet said, "Learning is mandatory for all men and women".

THINKING

One of the gifts of Allah to mankind is intellectual ability. This is because mankind has been created free, and has been given freedom of mind and choices. Mankind has the ability to think and to ponder. The art of thinking and pondering is only possible with freedom of mind. This means that Allah intended to have humans act, think and ponder freely. Without this ability of thinking and questioning, we will not be able to find Him or the Truth. The story of Prophet Abraham is a case in point in which he knew his position as a Prophet but he questioned the existence of God. The Qur'an clearly narrates this story as follows:

وَكَذَٰلِكَ نُرِىٓ إِبْرَٰهِيمَ مَلَكُوتَ ٱلسَّمَٰوَٰتِ وَٱلْأَرْضِ وَلِيَكُونَ مِنَ ٱلْمُوقِنِينَ (٧٥) فَلَمَّا جَنَّ عَلَيْهِ ٱلَّيْلُ رَءَا كَوْكَبًا قَالَ هَٰذَا رَبِّىْ فَلَمَّآ أَفَلَ قَالَ لَآ أُحِبُّ ٱلْءَافِلِينَ (٧٦) فَلَمَّا رَءَا ٱلْقَمَرَ بَازِغًا قَالَ هَٰذَا رَبِّىْ فَلَمَّآ أَفَلَ قَالَ لَئِن لَّمْ يَهْدِنِى رَبِّى لَأَكُونَنَّ مِنَ ٱلْقَوْمِ ٱلضَّآلِّينَ (٧٧) فَلَمَّا رَءَا ٱلشَّمْسَ بَازِغَةً قَالَ هَٰذَا رَبِّى هَٰذَآ أَكْبَرُ فَلَمَّآ أَفَلَتْ قَالَ يَٰقَوْمِ إِنِّى بَرِىٓءٌ مِّمَّا تُشْرِكُونَ (٧٨) إِنِّى وَجَّهْتُ وَجْهِىَ لِلَّذِى فَطَرَ ٱلسَّمَٰوَٰتِ وَٱلْأَرْضَ حَنِيفًا وَمَآ أَنَا۠ مِنَ ٱلْمُشْرِكِينَ (٧٩

"And so too did we show Abraham the celestial majesty and divine authority in the vast kingdom of the heavens and the earth, so he will be of those who believe in Allah with certainty.

So when the night spread over him, he saw a star, he said: This is my Lord! Then when it disappeared, he said, I do not love that which disappears.

So when he saw the moon rising he said: This is my Lord! Then when it disappeared, he said: If my lord does not guide me, I shall most surely be of the people who are astray.

So when he saw the sun rising, he said: This is my Lord! This is the greater of both of them! Then when it disappeared, he said :O my people! I'm innocent of worshiping all that you associate as gods with God.

I have turned my face, being ever upright of heart, to the One who alone originated the heavens and the earth and I am not of those who associate gods with God" (Qur'an 6:75-79).

Also,

Prophet Abraham questioned Allah about His power and how He gives life to the dead. The Qur'an states,

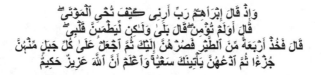

"And behold! Abraham said: My Lord! Show me how You give life to the dead. God said: Do you not believe? Abraham said: I do indeed! But it is only that my heart may be fully assured. He said: Take, then, four varied types of birds and draw them to you. Then set on each mountaintop a part of them. Then call them. They shall come rushing to you. And know, then, with certainty that God is, indeed, overpowering, all-wise" (Qur'an 2:260).

The above two verses in the story of Prophet Abraham pondering about the existence of God and power of God tells us that Allah wanted mankind to not believe in Him blindly and become certain of the Truth by questioning things. In this context, Abraham, actually led the foundation of research within humanity. Research is to question, find the truth, and express the facts. He proved to himself that not only God exists, but also He has power over all things. The Qur'an repeatedly asks mankind to think and to ponder about variety of issues in order to reach facts for themselves because accepting any theories or ideas without knowledge leads mankind astray and into darkness, ignorance, and fanaticism. The Qur'an communicates to the Prophet saying,

قُلْ هَلْ يَسْتَوِى ٱلْأَعْمَىٰ وَٱلْبَصِيرُ أَفَلَا تَتَفَكَّرُونَ

"Are the blind and the seeing equal? Will you not, then, reflect on the signs of God?" (Qur'an 6:50).

And also about thinking, the Qur'an asks people to comprehend and to think, saying,

وَإِذْ قَتَلْتُمْ نَفْسًا فَٱدَّٰرَأْتُمْ فِيهَا ۖ وَٱللَّهُ مُخْرِجٌ مَّا كُنتُمْ تَكْتُمُونَ

"So we said: "Strike the (body) with a piece of the (heifer)." Thus Allah brings the dead to life and shows you His signs: Perchance you may understand (think)" (Quran 2:72).

OBSERVING

Observing is a principle of learning and cognitive development to find the facts in truth. By observing, we distinguish right from wrong. As the Qur'an says,

وَمَا لَهُم بِهِۦ مِنْ عِلْمٍ ۖ إِن يَتَّبِعُونَ إِلَّا ٱلظَّنَّ ۖ وَإِنَّ ٱلظَّنَّ لَا يُغْنِى مِنَ ٱلْحَقِّ شَيْئًا

"But they have no knowledge therein. They follow nothing but conjecture: and conjecture avails nothing against truth" (Qur'an 53:28).

As we said, everything is founded and based upon pure knowledge. As the Qur'an says,

وَأَنَّ ٱللَّهَ قَدْ أَحَاطَ بِكُلِّ شَىْءٍ عِلْمًا

"Allah alone has truly encompassed all things in knowledge" (Qur'an 65:12).

Psychologically, observation leads us to curiosity and to learn to find facts about the "Truth". The "Truth" meaning finding the reasons of our creation through observation. By finding the truth for what He intends for us, we acknowledge our own existence within His creation. For instance, when we look at other humans, animals, plants, or insects, there must be a Creator for all living organisms. As the Qur'an says,

هُوَ ٱلَّذِى خَلَقَ لَكُم مَّا فِى ٱلْأَرْضِ جَمِيعًا ثُمَّ ٱسْتَوَىٰٓ إِلَى ٱلسَّمَآءِ فَسَوَّىٰهُنَّ سَبْعَ سَمَٰوَٰتٍ وَهُوَ بِكُلِّ شَىْءٍ عَلِيمٌ

"It is He Who had created for you all things that are on earth; moreover His design comprehends the heavens, for He gives orders and perfection to the seven firmaments; of all things He has perfect knowledge" (Qur'an 2:29).

From an Islamic psychological point of view, the only way to understand, comprehend, and acknowledge the fact of creation is through *"Iman"* (faith). The Qur'an says,

وَلَٰكِنَّ ٱللَّهَ حَبَّبَ إِلَيْكُمُ ٱلْإِيمَٰنَ وَزَيَّنَهُۥ فِى قُلُوبِكُمْ

"But Allah has endeared faith to you, and adorned it in your hearts" (Qur'an 49:7).

Allah guide us in Verse 30, Chapter 21, that we are not keen enough to observe His creation, for He says,

أَوَلَمْ يَرَ ٱلَّذِينَ كَفَرُوٓاْ أَنَّ ٱلسَّمَٰوَٰتِ وَٱلْأَرْضَ كَانَتَا رَتْقًا فَفَتَقْنَٰهُمَاۖ وَجَعَلْنَا مِنَ ٱلْمَآءِ كُلَّ شَىْءٍ حَىٍّ أَفَلَا يُؤْمِنُونَ

"Do not the unbelievers see that the heavens and the earth were joined together (as one unit of creation), before we clove them asunder, we made from water every living thing. Will they not then believe". (Qur'an 21:30).

The late Dr. Maurice Bucaille (1920-1998), in his most famous book, *The Bible, the Qur'an, and Science*, (English version 1979), writes, "The notion of 'getting something out of something' does not give rise to any doubts. The phrase can equally mean that every living thing was made of water (as its essential component) or that every living thing originated in water. The two possible meanings are strictly in accordance with scientific data. Life is in fact of aquatic origin and water is the major component of all living cells. Without water, life is not possible. When the possibility of life on another planet is discussed, the first question is always: does it contain sufficient quantity of water to support life?" [27]

The above verse in the scientific statement of Dr. Bucaille tells us the relationship of science and faith as well as our observation for finding the truth as mentioned above.

LEARNING

Islam encourages learning by and through the applications of the Qur'an and the traditions of the Prophet Muhammad, because the Prophet was, and still, is a role model for true Muslim behavior. So Muslims do not have any other choice of behavior, unless they are deviant. Following the footsteps of the Prophet, one believes that they will achieve felicity, progress, and peace of mind. If they do not do so, they become responsible for those actions. If the actions are not for the wellbeing of selves or for the community, they are considered to be deviant, and if the actions are good enough for themselves and for the community, they are considered to be pious. That is why the Prophet Muhammad teaches that Muslim children should be taught prayers and manners from age seven. Pedagogy studies show that the earlier you teach children the norm, values and manners, it is easier for them to grasp. "According to research, the first five years are important for the developmental of the child's brain, and the first three years are the most crucial in shaping the child's brain architecture. Early experiences provide the base for the brain's organizational developmental and functioning throughout life. They have a direct impact on how children develop learning skills as well as social and emotional abilities." [28]

According to Islamic pedagogy, there are acquired knowledge that people learn as a profession and there is the mode of behavior that people learn from the Prophet Muhammad. This is important in the study of learning, compared to western civilization, in which every family has it's own way of upbringing, while a Muslim family is required to bring up the child with the manner and values according to the role model of the Prophet. For example, respecting parents is not a choice. As long as parents are not deviant, and they do not commit an immoral act, a child is learned to respect them regardless of their social and economic status. Another example, is the relationship between a student and a teacher. Teachers need to be respected because they are molding a personality for a child. Children are required to pray for the well-being of not only their parents, but also for their teachers. Three people play a role for a child: the father, the mother, and the teacher. These three are the main source of a child's developmental behavior. Teachers are not only teaching subject matters but they are also a role model of conduct, behavior, values, dignity, and integrity. Learning also comes from the elderly, such as grandparents, due to their life experiences. Children learn the art of living through different narrations of their grandparents life experiences, which teach them how to cope with different situations, how to tackle and solve problems and how to avoid calamities and distress during times of difficulties. So children are brought up by a team effort of society and the goal is that the child becomes a productive member of not only their family, but of society as well. Story- telling for children is another tool of learning that makes children think and makes them curious enough to ask more questions. The Prophet of Islam has a famous saying that says, "Learning is mandatory for all men and women". Learning is not a subject matter; learning is more comprehensive in Islamic families and societies. Learning is behavior, cooperation, patience, support, feedback, and covers all aspects of life that an individual will experience or cope with in this life. For example, decision-making at an early age of sixteen and learning cooperation with other family members is a learning process for the future of the child. One of the most important aspects of learning is compassion to children, not to spoil them, but to give them the right feedback and support to be God oriented, responsible, and upright in thinking, so one day, they should be able to make sound decisions when their parents and family members are not there anymore, and the children become capable to lead others the way they were led by the previous generation.

According to psychologists, the definition of cognitive development "is the construction of thought processes, including remembering, problem solving, and decision-making, from childhood through adolescence to adulthood".[29] Muslim behavior is based upon that definition, however, that source of learning is not from the individual experiences alone but also from the role model and maxims of Prophet Muhammad. When it comes to decision-making everyone has their own ideas, but the Qur'an dictates that people should consult among themselves as well. The Qur'an also says that people are different in their words and the Prophet Muhammad said that the difference of opinion is a blessing of his community. The junction between the Qur'an and the hadith is a good tool of learning and decision-making. A Muslim should consult in all matters, with others, and at the same time, respect other people's opinions and consider the community and social affairs based upon their consultations and feedback to make a sound decision. This style of learning and decision-making reduces a lot of burden from the shoulder of one person in the family or in society.

Thinking requires learning. The Qur'an asks mankind,

$$وَقُل رَّبِّ زِدْنِى عِلْمًا$$

"O my Lord! Advance me in knowledge" (Qur'an 20:114).

So it becomes an obligation for every single person to strive for the sake of knowledge. Knowledge facilitates all aspects of life. It was intended by Allah that mankind should use the power of learning for his advancement. Allah says in the Qur'an,

$$ٱلَّذِى عَلَّمَ بِٱلْقَلَمِ (٤) عَلَّمَ ٱلْإِنسَـٰنَ مَا لَمْ يَعْلَمْ (٥)$$

"He who taught the use of the pen and "taught man that which he knew not" (Qur'an 96:4 - 5).

According to Islam, the whole universe is a unified system inseparable in its components. Therefore, science, faith, mankind, and the universe are all one and all have originated from Allah. It was because of this principle and association of faith and science that between 900-1200 A.D. Muslim scholars did most of the scientific works in the areas of mathematics, astronomy, physics, medicine, and geography. Based upon the Qur'an, Prophet Muhammad was a great promoter of knowledge. He said, "Seek knowledge, even in China". The phrase "even in China" means that learning and education does not recognize borders. Knowledge is universal and should be acquired anytime, anywhere. In another hadith he said, "seek knowledge from the cradle to the grave". The phrase "cradle to grave" implies that learning is a continuous never-ending process. One should always be in touch with the sources of learning and there is a law who is the *Rab* of all humanity. *Rab* (Lord) means that Allah is the source of learning and we learn from Him. The Hadith, mentioned above, also eliminates age and relation to learning. Men and women should be in touch with sources of knowledge throughout their entire life, otherwise they lose the motivation for life and their mind becomes stagnant. The purpose of learning is physical and spiritual. The physical part of learning is when we explore the world for our use, while spiritual learning is to polish our hearts and mind for a peaceful living within our lifespan. Also, the purpose of learning in this life is to transform the individual from a state of unconsciousness to that of consciousness. The Prophet, as a role model, guided Muslims to morality and ethical values and made the *Ummah* (Muslim community) know themselves. He said, "He who knows himself knows God". Therefore, the social and psychological consciousness in a person in Islam is with recognition within oneself. Allah acknowledges men/women of knowledge by saying,

وَإِذَا قِيلَ ٱنشُزُواْ فَٱنشُزُواْ يَرْفَعِ ٱللَّهُ ٱلَّذِينَ ءَامَنُواْ مِنكُمْ وَٱلَّذِينَ أُوتُواْ ٱلْعِلْمَ دَرَجَٰتٍ

"And when you are told to rise up; rise up: God will raise up to a suitable ranks (and degrees) those of you who believe and who have been granted knowledge" (Qur'an 58:11).

TRAVELING

When we look at human history closely, we can see that all civilization has developed when people moved from point A to point B. By moving from point A to point B, we mean that people move from a place of birth and resettle somewhere else. In our contemporary era, we do not need to resettle unless there is an acute need for resettlement, such as political turmoil, economic disaster, and social tyranny. However, people must travel to see the world, be exposed to diverse cultures, and learn different languages to understand the depth of human diversity and existence. That means traveling and migration is part of human development, and without that, humanity will be stagnant and not follow the path of progress. Staying in one place without exploring other lands, geography, and culture will make a person narrow-minded. Narrow-mindedness leads to fanaticism, ethnocentrism, and discrimination. The Qur'an says,

يَـٰٓأَيُّهَا ٱلنَّاسُ إِنَّا خَلَقْنَـٰكُم مِّن ذَكَرٍ وَأُنثَىٰ وَجَعَلْنَـٰكُمْ شُعُوبًا وَقَبَآئِلَ لِتَعَارَفُوٓا۟ إِنَّ أَكْرَمَكُمْ عِندَ ٱللَّهِ أَتْقَىٰكُمْ إِنَّ ٱللَّهَ عَلِيمٌ خَبِيرٌ

"O mankind! We created you from a single (pair) of a male and a female, and made you into nations and tribes, that you may know each other (not that you may despise each other). Verily the most honored of you in the sight of Allah is (he who is) the most righteous of you. And Allah has full knowledge and is well acquainted (with all things)" (Qur'an 49:13).

The above verse speaks of diversity among people of the world, that they are all one creation and we have to respect each other, learn how to live with each other, and create harmonious and peaceful coexistence. The Qur'an also says,

قُلْ سِيرُوا۟ فِى ٱلْأَرْضِ فَٱنظُرُوا۟ كَيْفَ بَدَأَ ٱلْخَلْقَ ثُمَّ ٱللَّهُ يُنشِئُ ٱلنَّشْأَةَ ٱلْأَخِرَةَ إِنَّ ٱللَّهَ عَلَىٰ كُلِّ شَىْءٍ قَدِيرٌ

"Travel through the earth and see how Allah did originate creation; so will Allah produce a later creation: For Allah has power over all things" (Qur'an 29:20).

The above verse clearly requires human beings to travel for their own development and see the wonders of the world that He created. I was born and raised in a land-locked country, but when I went to Europe for the first time and saw the ocean, it really made me closer to Allah, seeing His bounties for humanity. There are many wonders in the world that astonish you when you travel and we learn out of it for our own personal growth. Yusuf Ali, the interpreter of the Qur'an in the English language, writes in his commentary about the wonders of the world, saying, "But wonders upon wonders are disclosed the constitution of the matter itself, the atom, and the forces of energy, and in the distinction of animals, and the minds and capacities of man. And there is no limit to these things. Worlds upon worlds are created and transformed every moment, within and presumably beyond mans vision. From what we know we can judge of the unknown". (Abdullah Yusuf Ali, the Holy Qur'an translation and commentary, p. 1033). Development of mind is a cognitive psychological principle. In this area, just reading books or going to college is not adequate when we deal with human development in the arena of mind. *Iman* (faith) as a cognitive principle plays a major role in human development. That is why Allah introduced many prophets to introduce *Iman* and intellectualize humanity. "*Iman* (faith), it should be said in conclusion, is not merely an ethical category, Indeed, it is firstly, a cognitive category. That is to say, it has to do with knowledge, with the truthfulness of its propositions. And since the nature of its proposition content is a first principle of logic and knowledge of metaphysics, of ethics and aesthetics, it follows that it acts in the subject as a light that illuminates everything. As Al Ghazali describes, "*Iman* is a vision that puts all other dates and facts in the perspective, which is propers to, and requisite for, a true understanding of them. It is the grounding for a rational interpretation of the universe, it itself is the prime principle of reason cannot be non-rational or irrational and hence in contradiction with itself. It indeed is the first principle of rationality. To deny or oppose it is to lapse from reasonableness and hence from humanity". [30]

MEMORY AND AGING

It is very understandable and natural that all elements in the physical body, not only ages, but slowly and naturally deteriorates. Memory is part of that is. However, Muslim scientists in the past believed that reading is good for memory. Their argument was based on the fact that the Qur'an as an intellectual property; it affects the mind and the heart, and the first word revealed to Prophet Muhammad by Archangel Gabriel at the cave of Hira was to read. This "reading" has a vast intellectual implication in Islamic life. It was not only commanded to Prophet Muhammad to read the revelation, but the first revelation alludes to humanity that the only way to succeed in this life is through reading and knowledge. Psychologically, reading enhances not only knowledge but sharpens the memory. Reading and engaging the brain with positive activities keeps the memory more intact.

We should bear in mind that there is a difference between loss of memory, due to aging, and brain disease, such as dementia and Alzheimer's that could be genetic and the brain may have some plagues from past generations. Loss of memory due to aging is a natural process, while brain disease may take place even before 65.

All psychological trends, such as isolation and depression, take place in the elderly due to lack of spirituality. Faith is a very strong tool to protect one from all psychological negative impacts. Of course, when we are talking of faith in psychology we mean a total submission to the will of God according to Islamic culture. Just being a Muslim by name is not good enough to avoid dilemmas.

Muslim societies have great responsibilities towards their elderly. The elderly in a Muslim family is not the responsibility of nursing homes or any other individuals outside the family but that of the family itself. It is a religious responsibility for each member of the family to take care of the elderly. It is reciprocal relationship between parents and children that in the beginning of life of a family, a child is taken care of by parents. The same child should take care of his parents in their old age. In Islam, this is not family responsibility but a religious duty to those who commit to themselves and claim to be Muslim. Respect of parents, require that children at any age, are not supposed to say even a word or sound of contempt towards their parents.

The core principle of any civilized society is to care about one another. In an Islamic society, this care begins at home where our personalities are developed and parents play a major role in upbringing their children. Parents' attention to educating to their children will have three impacts. First, upbringing a moral individual; second, establishing a healthy family, and third, contributing to a healthy society. It is because of this noble contribution of parents that Islam places a strong emphasis on respecting parents, caring about them in their old age, and honoring them. In Islam, parents are the building blocks of a healthy social system.

One role of education in Islam is to promote recognition of each others' rights and to develop a sense of mutual respect for each other. This concept of mutual respect comes through a sense of responsibility toward God and the Prophet. Manners, which are part of education, are taught from childhood. The codes of conduct that dictate these manners come directly from the teaching of the Prophet. The Prophet is the mentor for every single member of the family. His teachings are taken very seriously. It is not optional. This is because Muslims believe that by following the footsteps of the Prophet, they can achieve felicity toward performing acts of goodness in this world and gain paradise in the Hereafter. It is with this culture that a Muslim's personality is developed. The dignity of a Muslim individual in the family as well as in society is to live with respect, extend respect, and cherish people with respect.

The respect and care for parents and the elderly is not only a social responsibility, but also a divine command that Muslims must follow. Otherwise they will be seriously accountable in the Hereafter for violating this basic human right. The Qur'an says,

وَقَضَىٰ رَبُّكَ أَلَّا تَعْبُدُوٓا إِلَّآ إِيَّاهُ وَبِٱلْوَٰلِدَيْنِ إِحْسَٰنًا إِمَّا يَبْلُغَنَّ عِندَكَ ٱلْكِبَرَ أَحَدُهُمَآ أَوْ كِلَاهُمَا فَلَا تَقُل لَّهُمَآ أُفٍّ وَلَا

تَنْهَرْهُمَا وَقُل لَّهُمَا قَوْلًا كَرِيمًا (٢٣) وَٱخْفِضْ لَهُمَا جَنَاحَ ٱلذُّلِّ مِنَ ٱلرَّحْمَةِ وَقُل رَّبِّ ٱرْحَمْهُمَا كَمَا رَبَّيَانِى صَغِيرًا (

٢٤) رَّبُّكُمْ أَعْلَمُ بِمَا فِى نُفُوسِكُمْ إِن تَكُونُوا صَٰلِحِينَ فَإِنَّهُۥ كَانَ لِلْأَوَّٰبِينَ غَفُورًا (٢٥)

Thy Lord hath decreed that you worship none but Him, and that you be kind to your parents. When one or both of them attain old age in thy life, say not to them a word of contempt, nor repel them, but address them in terms of honor. And out of kindness, lower to them the wing of humility, and say My Lord! Bestow on them Thy Mercy even as they cherished me in childhood. Your Lord knows best what is in your hearts: If you do deeds of righteousness, verily, He is most forgiving to those who turn to Him again and again (in true repentance). (Qur'an 17: 23-25)

The above verse clearly shows man's responsibility to the Creator. This verse teaches humility and respect toward parents who raise their children, and require the children to be responsible toward and to cherish their parents and even ask God for their well-being. The Prophet of Islam said that after death, there are three things that remain behind. First, knowledge that other people learn from and that would serve as guidance. Second, charity that sustains its effect, and third, a righteous child who prays for his/her parents during their lifetime and after their lifetime.

Men and women of faith rely on God's guidance and the Prophet's teachings. Kindness, support, help in time of need, and praying for parents is the responsibility of each Muslim, particularly in their old age. A noble act that is pleasing to the Almighty Creator is to be kind to one's parents.

It is understood through the Qur'an that if mankind forgets Allah, He will forget them. This means that in order to enhance memory according to the teachings of Islam one has to remember God constantly and praise Him in the heart. This praising the Lord of universe will improve, it is believed, the conscious and the mind. The Qur'an says,

$$\text{أَذْكُرُونِيَ أَذْكُرْكُمْ وَاشْكُرُواْ لِى وَلَا تَكْفُرُونِ}$$

"Therefore, remember Me, and, I will remember you, be grateful to Me and never deny Me". (Qur'an 2:152).

In this verse, there is a direct relation between remembering of God and faith. A combination of the two will enhance the purity of heart and sharpness of mind. In mystic life, the remembering of God is called Zikr, which "represents both a solemn ritual and spiritual state of mind and heart, in which the devotee seeks to realize the presence of God. Thus, there is Zikr of the mind and Zikr of the heart. For beginners, the one may lead to the other, but in many cases the two may be simultaneous. There is a subtler distinction between the Zikr that is open, and the Zikr that is secret. Corresponding to the two doors of the heart, the fleshly and in the spiritual". (The Interpretation of Yusuf Ali, p. 61). It is understood that both reading and Zikr will have worldly, spiritual, and heavenly impact on an individual as a creation of God. God, according to the Qur'an, is ever unmindful of His Creation, mankind included. The Qur'an says,

$$\text{وَمَا اللَّهُ بِغَافِلٍ عَمَّا تَعْمَلُونَ}$$

"And God is not unmindful of what you do" (Qur'an 2:149).

This is another Qur'anic proof that God is constantly watching over us not for any restriction because mankind has been created free, but watching to see that we achieve our goal and objectives with His mighty support and care.

HUMANISM

Mankind has been created free. The Qur'an is simply a guide to mankind, but since He created mankind, He warns them of the danger of falling into the state of disbelief, which could make human beings like an astronaut floating in space without a tether. Nevertheless, God does not impose His commands on mankind and lets him find his way for prosperity and felicity in this world and in the Hereafter. Professor Boisard in his very eloquent book, *Humanism in Islam,* writes, "When considering religion in the three etymological meanings of the word, we find that Islam presupposes on the one hand voluntary preference, of free choice to surrender to Allah and to moral and cultural rules, on the other hand it implies the collection and preservation of a true human heritage. It specifically and ultimately defines the position of the believer and relation to the absolute as well as relations of solidarity among men. It is in this way that Islam appears as a uniform social and political fact, as an observable historic phenomenon in short, as a civilization which has its own conception of man and his place in society in which has been put forward certain axioms determining relations between peoples". [31]

According to Islam, mankind should not be a fatalist with irrational minds. On the contrary, mankind is made responsible for all actions and thoughts, as vicegerents of God on earth. In other words, mankind is carrying God's mission on earth and takes the responsibility of His creation to conduct justice, exploration for the meliority of life, coexistence, and protection of His creations that He has bestowed upon us as a trust. Many people misunderstand Islamic philosophy, intellectuality, and wrongfully think that Muslims only rely on the Divine will without using their intellect for human affairs, which is not the case at all in Islam. The Qur'an rejects the idea that we rely only on the Divine will and that people have no rationality of their own. The Qur'anic verse says,

إِنَّا عَرَضْنَا ٱلْأَمَانَةَ عَلَى ٱلسَّمَـٰوَٰتِ وَٱلْأَرْضِ وَٱلْجِبَالِ فَأَبَيْنَ أَن يَحْمِلْنَهَا وَأَشْفَقْنَ مِنْهَا وَحَمَلَهَا ٱلْإِنسَـٰنُ إِنَّهُۥ كَانَ ظَلُومًا جَهُولًا (٧٢)

"We did indeed offer the trust to the heavens and the earth and the mountains but they refused to undertake it, being afraid thereof: but man undertook it" (Qur'an 33:72).

This verse from the Qur'an tells us that mankind has been given the responsibility of the earth, the protection of the earth, and the survival of the earth with the blessing and guidance from the God Almighty. According to the Qur'an, mankind is a representative of God on earth. So, with the freedom of the mind, intellect, having the responsibility of the earth, and being a representative of God on earth gives mankind a whole range of power to conduct affairs with a free will. However, they are ultimately responsible for their actions as well. Muslim humanistic psychologists, like any other humanistic psychologists, use their rational minds to solve problems and learn from experiences and ideas, but the ultimate goal is justice and peace for everyone.

In Islamic psychology, determinism, which are actions determined by external factors, and free will are both tied together. According to Islam, people have a free will and mankind is created with free will. Because of that, man has the power to control outside forces individually, if not collectively. For example, someone makes another angry, it is in the individual's potential to not get angry and control that outside force. If outside forces are negative, that naturally produces negative energy in us. Our challenge according to the Qur'an is to counteract negative energy with positive energy. In other words, we have to answer bad with good according to the Qur'an.

FATALISM

There is a misconception about Islamic cultural principles where many people misunderstand the Muslim belief system such as that they do not have a role in anything and everything is predetermined by God. Fatalism is defined as follows: "The belief that all events are predetermined and therefore inevitable" (Google definition).

As a matter of fact, God almighty granted mankind intellect, talent, sagacity, common sense, and an ability, to find the truth for themselves, and to move on. Muslims are not fatalists, because these five gifts that God has granted them, enable them to influence the course of history and change themselves. The Qur'an says,

إِنَّ ٱللَّهَ لَا يُغَيِّرُ مَا بِقَوْمٍ حَتَّىٰ يُغَيِّرُواْ مَا بِأَنفُسِهِمْ

"Allah will not change the condition of a people until they change what is in themselves" (Qur'an 13:11). In another verse, Allah says,

وَأَن لَّيْسَ لِلْإِنسَٰنِ إِلَّا مَا سَعَىٰ

"That man can have nothing but what he strives for" (Qur'an 53:39).

To make our point more clear about fatalism, man is responsible for his own actions. The Qur'an says,

مَّنِ اَهْتَدَىٰ فَإِنَّمَا يَهْتَدِى لِنَفْسِهِ وَمَن ضَلَّ فَإِنَّمَا يَضِلُّ عَلَيْهَا وَلَا تَزِرُ وَازِرَةٌ وِزْرَ أُخْرَىٰ وَمَا كُنَّا مُعَذِّبِينَ حَتَّىٰ نَبْعَثَ

رَسُولاً

"Whoever is guided is only guided for (the benefit of) his soul. And whoever errs only errs against it. And no bearer of burdens will bear the burden of another. And never would We punish until We sent a messenger" (Qur'an 17:15).

What is predetermined is not on the hands of mankind but rather on the hands of the Creator and that is our birth, earthquakes, floods, and our death. Mankind can play a major role in changing societies for the sake of peace, justice, progress, and exploration of those gifted things that are for their usage. Fatalism is not an Islamic phenomenon for daily life of humanity.

DESTINY:

Destiny of mankind, as far as their last day in this world, what age they will depart, what sustenance they may have in their lifetime, what calamities they may be exposed in his lifetime; all these are examples of destiny that mankind has no power over. However, during the process, mankind has the ability to change his destiny in the right direction. For example, a thief decides to not steal anymore, to repent, and be contempt to what he has and will never do wrong again. By principle, it is him who changed his life, but Allah knows that he has changed his life. Mankind changes throughout the process of life and experiences from his encounters and from his environmental surroundings. What is important in predestination, psychologically, is that mankind has certain control over their daily affairs. In some areas, they may have full control but they may not know the outcome of all their activities in the future.

PSYCHO-DYNAMICS

PSYCHO-DYNAMICS

Psycho-dynamics is the interrelation of the unconscious and conscious mental and emotional forces that determine personality and motivation. Theoretically, it is any theory "of behavior that emphasizes internal conflicts, motives, and unconscious forces". [32]

A person should be able to know themselves. They should know their desires, needs, strengths, and weaknesses. An individual has to believe in their Creator and rely on their Creator because their Creator knows the heart and minds of every single person. As the Qur'an says,

$$إِنَّ ٱللَّهَ عَلِيمٌ بِذَاتِ ٱلصُّدُورِ$$

"God knoweth well all the secrets of the heart" (Qur'an 3:119).

This means, after submission and recognition of the role of God in our lives, faith (iman), becomes a major psychological principle in Islamic life. It is through strong faith in the Creator that a human being aligns all their thoughts, actions, and consequently becomes at peace with the self and with others. The main reason that the "unconscious" gets disturbed, goes to the wrong direction, and causes damage to self and eventually to others is because the "self" forgets its own existence in relation with the Creator Who is the source of energy for motivation. However, God, has the source of energy and motivation for individual for the purpose of felicity, happiness, and achievement of individuals desires, goals, and objectives. This is because God is not the oppressor; it is we who oppress ourselves. The Qur'an says,

وَمَا ظَلَمَهُمُ ٱللَّهُ وَلَـٰكِنْ أَنفُسَهُمْ يَظْلِمُونَ

"And it is not God that hath wronged them, but they wronged themselves" (Qur'an 3:117).

The Qur'an also says,

وَهُوَ ظَالِمٌ لِّنَفْسِهِ قَالَ مَآ أَظُنُّ أَن تَبِيدَ هَٰذِهِ أَبَدًا

"In a state (of mind) unjust to his soul: he said, "I deem not that this will ever perish". (Qur'an 18:35).

The above two verses clearly indicate the fact that man is responsible for his own actions and is accountable not only to the Creator but also to society, and this is what socio-ethics is all about. Bakhtiar states,

"Psycho-dynamics theory in the area of psychological imbalances, separate from biological illnesses, tends to emphasize those aspects of the self that have to do with defense mechanism (cognitive in the system of psycho-ethics). In terms of psycho-ethics, it would be a person in the underdevelopment of the cognitive system. A person who is cognitively unconscious of the Presence of God in a state of disbelief". [33]

The comprehension is this that within a Muslim's mind, faith plays a major role in the psycho-dynamics of Islamic psychology. But what is faith? At this point, we have to define faith variously. Faith is the strong belief in God. Believing in God does not give us a total peace of mind unless we trust Him fully. Trust is the firm belief in the reliability, the truth, ability, and strength of Allah. Reciprocally, the concept of trust not only gives a person hope and reliability but makes them stronger in their legal, moral, and ethical desires. At the same time, since the trust is fully committed to the Creator and the individual strongly believes in Him, then the Creator reinforces his strength for achieving desired goals, which is why that faith in Allah and all aspects of life, being in the form of theo-ethics, socio-ethics, and psycho-ethics, is the cornerstone of well-being and a firm state of mind. However, this belief and trust should not be abused or taken for granted for wrong-doings that are against the will of Allah that harm humanity. Allah's intention for humanity is peace, justice, and harmony for all, regardless of faith, denominations, gender, race, religion, nationality, and culture.

Allah loves those who rely and trust in Him. Again this trust should not be abused as many people wrongfully do so. Allah says,

قُل لَّن يُصِيبَنَآ إِلَّا مَا كَتَبَ ٱللَّهُ لَنَا هُوَ مَوۡلَىٰنَاۚ وَعَلَى ٱللَّهِ فَلۡيَتَوَكَّلِ ٱلۡمُؤۡمِنُونَ

"Say nothing will happen to us except what God has decreed for us: He is our Protector, and in God let the Believers put their trust" (Qur'an 9:51).

And,

فَإِذَا عَزَمۡتَ فَتَوَكَّلۡ عَلَى ٱللَّهِۚ إِنَّ ٱللَّهَ يُحِبُّ ٱلۡمُتَوَكِّلِّ

"Put thy trust in God. For God loves those who put their trust (in Him) (Qur'an 3:159).

This verse constitutes the theory of psycho-dynamics of Islamic psychology.

DISEASES OF THE HEART

According to the Qur'an, mankind is superior to all creatures, but mankind is also a synthesis of good and bad qualities. Good qualities such as love, empathy, compassion, and kindness, and bad qualities such as envy, ill-thinking, filthy desires, jealousy, and hatred all give human beings a sense of struggle within himself and towards society. In this chapter, we will explore the bad qualities of mankind from a psychological point of view and its impact on individuals in societies at large. It's also important to note that mankind is responsible for

105

their thoughts and actions, good or bad. Nurturing bad thoughts will eventually make a person a sociopath simply because they have not been trained properly for a good understanding of the art of living, being a good person, being a productive individual, and supportive/cooperative person.

Sociologically, the diseases of the heart are not a natural phenomenon, but are due to the circumstances of how a child was raised, the economic standing of the family, and other social factors that were neglected during early childhood, which makes a person the way they are. There's a difference between Islamic culture and an un-Islamic culture, in that the former can be acquired at any age. By doing so, one can change lifestyle, vision, worldview, manners, and behavior just by whole-heartedly accepting the Islamic faith as a way of life.

In the United States, there are about three million students in middle and high school who are suspended annually and the educational system takes different approaches to correct the situations, but have always failed. The disciplinary actions for correcting student's manners and behavior in school failed to a point that students have become violent. The point is, that these students were not given the proper intellectual training from adolescence to teenager years in order to be prepared for larger roles of their lives in the future. Students without spiritual/intellectual training for a civil life or according to Islamic psychological principles, spiritual training, would have a "blank slate".

As stated earlier, Omar Khatab, the second *khalif*, before accepting Islam, was a high tempered and a stubborn person. After accepting Islam, he became very tender-hearted and he earned the title of "*Faruq*", meaning that he was the most just when dealing with people. So this is an example of the effort of Islamic manners, behaviors, and cultures acquired by imitating the role modeling of the Prophet.

Muslims believe that the heart is the house of God. This means, that as long as we keep His name in our hearts, remember Him, and follow His commands as human beings we will be on the right path, if and only if things are understood properly and moderately based upon the traditions of the Prophet. If we happen to take God out of our heart, then the heart will be exposed to different diseases. The Qur'an beautifully says,

فِى قُلُوبِهِم مَّرَضٌ فَزَادَهُمُ ٱللَّهُ مَرَضًا ۖ وَلَهُمْ عَذَابٌ أَلِيمٌ بِمَا كَانُوا يَكْذِبُونَ

"In their hearts is a disease; and God has increased their disease and grievous is the penalty they (incur) because they are false (to themselves)" (Qur'an 2:10).

Yusuf Ali, the translator and interpreter of the Qur'an writes about this verse, "The insincere man who thinks like he can get the best of both worlds by compromising with good and evil only increases the disease of his heart, because he is not true to himself. Even the good, which comes to him he can pervert to evil. So the rain which fills out the ear of corn or lends fragrance to the rose also lends strength to the thorn or adds strength to the poison of the deadly night-shade". So man is responsible to be good since he has been provided a good intellectual and spiritual education and this is what Islamic psychologically is all about.

The following are the diseases of the heart that plague humans to the lowest of the low.

Jealousy: Disease of the heart that destroys an individual. God wants people to polish their hearts and stay away from jealousy and He asks people to pray and to stay away from those who envy, saying, "And from the mischief of the envious one as he practices envy" (Qur'an 113:5). To stay away from this disease is to trust God with purity of the heart.

Ill-Thinking: Disease of the heart that causes emotional and mental harm to an individual and even pushes others away due to the constant negativity of the mind.

Gossiping and Backbiting: Disease of the heart that shows the weakness of a person because they do not have the power of logic or sound-reasoning to accept others and they resort to backbiting and gossiping.

Suspicions and Assumptions: This leads to unjustified conclusions. Suspicions and assumptions mean that the heart is not polished enough for purification. Undue suspicion is a problem that leads to accusation and social disaster.

Spying: Spying on people without any legal justification is a disease of the heart. Spying can cause mistrust, fear, suspicion, assumption, and demeaning of others including transferring words from one to another. The Qur'an sums up the above illness of the heart in the following verse,

يَـٰٓأَيُّهَا ٱلَّذِينَ ءَامَنُوا۟ ٱجْتَنِبُوا۟ كَثِيرًا مِّنَ ٱلظَّنِّ إِنَّ بَعْضَ ٱلظَّنِّ إِثْمٌ ۖ وَلَا تَجَسَّسُوا۟ وَلَا يَغْتَب بَّعْضُكُم بَعْضًا ۚ أَيُحِبُّ أَحَدُكُمْ

أَن يَأْكُلَ لَحْمَ أَخِيهِ مَيْتًا فَكَرِهْتُمُوهُ ۚ وَٱتَّقُوا۟ ٱللَّهَ ۚ إِنَّ ٱللَّهَ تَوَّابٌ رَّحِيمٌ

"Oh you who believe! Avoid suspicion as much (as possible): for suspicion in some cases is

a sin: and spy not on each other nor speak ill of each other behind their backs. Would any of you like to eat the flesh of his dead brother? No, you would abhor it…but fear God: for God is Oft-Returning, Most Merciful" (Qur'an 49:12).

Accusation: Accusing someone for wrongdoing without any evidence or witnesses could lead to ill consequences and damage relationships between people. In the history of Islam, Aisha, the beloved wife of the Prophet Muhammad, was accused of wrongdoing by the hypocrites until a verse was revealed stating her innocence:

إِنَّ ٱلَّذِينَ جَآءُو بِٱلْإِفْكِ عُصْبَةٌ مِّنكُمْ ۚ لَا تَحْسَبُوهُ شَرًّا لَّكُم ۖ بَلْ هُوَ خَيْرٌ لَّكُمْ ۚ لِكُلِّ ٱمْرِئٍ مِّنْهُم مَّا ٱكْتَسَبَ مِنَ ٱلْإِثْمِ ۚ وَٱلَّذِى

تَوَلَّىٰ كِبْرَهُۥ مِنْهُمْ لَهُۥ عَذَابٌ عَظِيمٌ (١١) لَّوْلَآ إِذْ سَمِعْتُمُوهُ ظَنَّ ٱلْمُؤْمِنُونَ وَٱلْمُؤْمِنَـٰتُ بِأَنفُسِهِمْ خَيْرًا وَقَالُوا۟ هَـٰذَآ إِفْكٌ

مُّبِينٌ (١٢) لَّوْلَا جَآءُو عَلَيْهِ بِأَرْبَعَةِ شُهَدَآءَ ۚ فَإِذْ لَمْ يَأْتُوا۟ بِٱلشُّهَدَآءِ فَأُو۟لَـٰٓئِكَ عِندَ ٱللَّهِ هُمُ ٱلْكَـٰذِبُونَ (١٣) وَلَوْلَا فَضْلُ

ٱللَّهِ عَلَيْكُمْ وَرَحْمَتُهُۥ فِى ٱلدُّنْيَا وَٱلْءَاخِرَةِ لَمَسَّكُمْ فِى مَآ أَفَضْتُمْ فِيهِ عَذَابٌ عَظِيمٌ (١٤) إِذْ تَلَقَّوْنَهُۥ بِأَلْسِنَتِكُمْ وَتَقُولُونَ

بِأَفْوَاهِكُم مَّا لَيْسَ لَكُم بِهِۦ عِلْمٌ وَتَحْسَبُونَهُۥ هَيِّنًا وَهُوَ عِندَ ٱللَّهِ عَظِيمٌ (١٥) وَلَوْلَآ إِذْ سَمِعْتُمُوهُ قُلْتُم مَّا يَكُونُ لَنَآ أَن

نَّتَكَلَّمَ بِهَٰذَا سُبْحَٰنَكَ هَٰذَا بُهْتَٰنٌ عَظِيمٌ (١٦) يَعِظُكُمُ ٱللَّهُ أَن تَعُودُوا۟ لِمِثْلِهِۦٓ أَبَدًا إِن كُنتُم مُّؤْمِنِينَ (١٧)وَيُبَيِّنُ ٱللَّهُ لَكُمُ

ٱلْءَايَٰتِ ۚ وَٱللَّهُ عَلِيمٌ حَكِيمٌ (١٨) إِنَّ ٱلَّذِينَ يُحِبُّونَ أَن تَشِيعَ ٱلْفَٰحِشَةُ فِى ٱلَّذِينَ ءَامَنُوا۟ لَهُمْ عَذَابٌ أَلِيمٌ فِى ٱلدُّنْيَا وَٱلْءَاخِرَةِ ۚ

وَٱللَّهُ يَعْلَمُ وَأَنتُمْ لَا تَعْلَمُونَ (١٩) وَلَوْلَا فَضْلُ ٱللَّهِ عَلَيْكُمْ وَرَحْمَتُهُۥ وَأَنَّ ٱللَّهَ رَءُوفٌ رَّحِيمٌ (٢٠)

"Verily those who brought forth the slander (against 'Aisha) are a group among you. Consider it not a bad thing for you. Nay, it is good for you. Unto every man among them will be paid that which he had earned of the sin, and as for him among them who had the greater share therein, his will be a great torment. (11). Why then, did not the believers, men and women, when you heard it (the slander), think good of their own people and say: "This (charge) is an obvious lie?" (12). Why did they not produce four witnesses? Since they (the slanderers) have not produced witnesses! Then with Allah they are the liars (13). Had it not been for the Grace of Allah and His Mercy unto you in this world and in the Hereafter, a great torment would have touched you for that whereof you had spoken (14). When you were propagating it with your tongues, and uttering with your mouths that whereof you had no knowledge, you counted it a little thing, while with Allah it was very great (15). And why did you not, when you heard it, say: "It is not right for us to speak of this. Glory be to You (O Allah)! This is a great lie." (16). Allah forbids you from it and warns you not to repeat the like of it forever, if you are believers (17). And Allah makes the Ayat (proofs, evidence, verses, lessons, signs, revelations, etc.) plain to you, and Allah is All-Knowing, All-Wise (18). Verily, those who like that (the crime of) illegal sexual intercourse should be propagated among those who believe, they will have a painful torment in this world and in the Hereafter. And Allah knows and you know not (19). And had it not been for the Grace of Allah and His Mercy on you, (Allah would have hastened the punishment upon you). And that Allah is full of Kindness, Most Merciful (20). (Qur'an 24:11-20).

Lying: Disease of the heart that becomes a norm for some people and they become pathetic liars who constantly lie and make others believe what is not true. This is due to social inferiority and lack of achievement. For example those who have not achieved something, tell lies about themselves create a fake manifestation of themselves. On the contrary, those who are achievers don't lie because their achievements owe evident, they let their success speak for themselves.

Hypocrisy: One's word is not what he really believes.

Sarcasm: Sarcasm has been defined in Merriam-Webster Dictionary as the "use of words that mean the opposite of what you really want to say especially to insult someone, to show irritation or to be funny". The Qur'an mentions about those who are sarcastic against people of faith, saying

يَـٰٓأَيُّهَا ٱلَّذِينَ ءَامَنُوا۟ لَا يَسْخَرْ قَوْمٌ مِّن قَوْمٍ عَسَىٰٓ أَن يَكُونُوا۟ خَيْرًا مِّنْهُمْ
وَلَا نِسَآءٌ مِّن نِّسَآءٍ عَسَىٰٓ أَن يَكُنَّ خَيْرًا مِّنْهُنَّ
وَلَا تَلْمِزُوٓا۟ أَنفُسَكُمْ وَلَا تَنَابَزُوا۟ بِٱلْأَلْقَـٰبِ
بِئْسَ ٱلِٱسْمُ ٱلْفُسُوقُ بَعْدَ ٱلْإِيمَـٰنِ
وَمَن لَّمْ يَتُبْ فَأُو۟لَـٰٓئِكَ هُمُ ٱلظَّـٰلِمُونَ

"O you who believe! Let not some men among you laugh at others: It may be that the (latter) are better than the (former): Nor let some women laugh at others: It may be that the (latter are better than the (former): Nor defame nor be sarcastic to each other, nor call each other by (offensive) nicknames: Ill-seeming is a name connoting wickedness, (to be used of one) after he has believed: And those who do not desist are (indeed) wrong-doing ones" (Qur'an 49:11).

Vulgar Language: Another disease of the heart is the use of vulgar language. It is considered an immoral act. Whatever we say, it comes from our heart and that is a reflection of our personality. It is extremely important to say things within that won't hurt others. This does not mean that one should not express his political or social views, but since Islam is a religion of justice, peace, and morality everything needs to be moral bound when expressed. That's why abusive language or vulgar language is a reflection of our heart and intention and is condemned in Islam. Prophet Muhammad said, "A believer is the one that people are safe from his words and his hands".

NAFS/EGO

We would like to define ego based on the principle of psychoanalysis, which is, "the part of the mind that mediates between the conscious and the unconscious and is responsible for reality testing and a sense of personal identity" (Google definition). However, ego, self or *nafs* according to Islamic terminology, is a tool for self-motivation, guidance, or self-destruction. We could also say that *nafs* is a "chip" in our mind that gears human beings toward different actions and interactions. This *nafs* makes a person who they are. *Nafs* leads a person to felicity, tranquility, and a desired personality, and if not controlled properly, it can mislead a person. This "chip" is connected to our mind, which is "human hardware". *Nafs* is the whole psychology of human being. If it leads to wrongdoing, it will upset the spirit "ruh" within us. *Nafs* is also connected to our intelligence for distinguishing good from bad or the truth from falsehood.

Nafs, as we said, is connected to the mind and to the heart. *Nafs* signals the mind and reflects to the heart, so it plays a major role within the relationship between the heart and the mind. *Nafs* can also easily pollute both the mind and the heart, and it is up to the individual's "aql" (intelligence) to use for controlling the *nafs* and protect the mind and the heart from evil. *Nafs*, as ego, is also, psychologically speaking, "self". The Qur'an says,

وَمَآ أُبَرِّئُ نَفْسِىٓ إِنَّ ٱلنَّفْسَ لَأَمَّارَةٌۢ بِٱلسُّوٓءِ إِلَّا مَا رَحِمَ رَبِّىٓ إِنَّ رَبِّى غَفُورٌ رَّحِيمٌ

"Nor do I absolve my own self (Of blame): the (human) self (nafs) is certainly prone to evil, unless my Lord do bestow His Mercy: but surely my Lord is Oft-Forgiving, most Merciful" (Qur'an 12:53).

The Qur'an speaks about *nafs al' Ammara* that is when "self" leads by the command of mind to evil, wrong doing, and eventually leads to destruction of the person. Evil or wrongdoing is forgetting the fact about one's priorities, goal, objective, values, and morals. For example, stealing is an example of *nafs al-Ammara*. Also, by the same token, breaking a trust is a consequence of *nafs al-Ammara*. The same *nafs* could change mode and leads to prosperity, felicity, happiness, and satisfaction. "It is, in fact, the lowest stage of spiritual growth of man. It is what one may one called his animal self; low desires and animal passions rule the mind, and he is capable of doing any evil without feeling any pangs at all. He submits to his carnal desires like the brute". [34]

Nafs has a tendency to either do good or bad. At the same time, because of this tendency, which constitutes human nature, he has the ability to move back and forth if he is a God- conscious person. The second stage is *nafs al' Lawwama*. At this stage, people do wrong, consciously or unconsciously, make mistakes, commit sins, but if they are God-conscious, they go back to the third stage and that is of certainty. The Qur'an says,

$$وَلَآ أُقْسِمُ بِٱلنَّفْسِ ٱللَّوَّامَةِ$$

"And I do call to witness the self-reproaching spirit: (eschew Evil)" (Qur'an 75:2).

If out of ego, one commits a major wrong-doing such as adultery, the solution is to repent and not commit that wrong again. But for minor mistakes, one needs to ask for forgiveness.

As the Qur'an says,

$$يَٰٓأَيَّتُهَا ٱلنَّفْسُ ٱلْمُطْمَئِنَّةُ (٢٧) ٱرْجِعِىٓ إِلَىٰ رَبِّكِ رَاضِيَةً مَّرْضِيَّةً (٢٨)$$

"To the righteous nafs will be said: "O (thou) nafs in (complete) rest and satisfaction! Come back to your Lord, well pleased (thyself), and well-pleasing unto Him" (Qur'an, 89:27-28).

This is the final stage of nafs that Allah expects from the believers. That they should become certain or at peace of their actions and deeds in the right way, this is called nafs al' Mutma' inna, which means a nafs or ego that rests with peace, certainty, and a God conscious mind that will never do wrong. Nafs al 'mutma'inna, or ego of certainty and peace, comes with total obedience of Allah for seeking righteousness. What is important about ego of certainty/peace is that a person does not live in suspicion, hypocrisy, and fear. This mode of ego will secure happiness in this world, and the self-will not fear neither people or in the Hereafter. Nafs provides a great challenge to humans for righteousness or wrongdoing or even in-between, because there are people who do wrong but they ask for repentance and forgiveness. As we mentioned earlier, nafs determines not only human personality, but also their identity. It is nafs that decides for one's social position in society. If one lies, cheats, breaks a truce, betrays others, it is all because of *nafs al-Ammara.* But if he is a man of righteousness and follows the path of goodness and felicity, then people would know him as such. "This *Imaan*, or faith, has two aspects: a *cognitive* aspect that recognizes and affirms the belief of Allah with conviction from the depth of the heart; and a *volitional (willful)* aspect that then surrenders to this affirmed Truth and places a complete trust in Allah. We should *recognize* the supremacy of Allah and then *willingly* act accordingly. In order to fully encompass both these aspects of Imaan, we need to strive hard and consciously monitor our own development and growth, and constantly reach to attain closeness to Allah by earning His pleasure"[35] This is how one can reach the stage of al'Mutma'inna.

The above three categories, al'Ammara, al 'lawamma, and al'mutma'inna, of nafs give us a better understanding of theo-ethics, socio-ethics, and psycho-ethics, all three stem from our nafs.

THEO-ETHICS

Theo-ethics establishes the relationship of self to his Creator. In this relationship, which is a deep conviction to Allah, determines a person's understanding of his position within the universal system. Allah created the whole universe and mankind is part of this universal system, and when mankind acknowledges His creation by Allah, then his theo-ethics develops within the following principles.

He acknowledges the fact that Allah is the Creator and he is the servant of Allah and obeys Him unconditionally.

Theo-ethics affirms and confirms that Allah is the guidance, the Provider, the Sustainer, the Protector, and Savior of the universe, mankind included.

The following verses from the Qur'an confirm the fact that anyone who breaks the covenant or rejects faith and ignore what Allah has created for mankind violates principles of theo-ethics.

ٱلَّذِينَ يَنقُضُونَ عَهْدَ ٱللَّهِ مِنۢ بَعْدِ مِيثَٰقِهِۦ وَيَقْطَعُونَ مَآ أَمَرَ ٱللَّهُ بِهِۦٓ أَن يُوصَلَ وَيُفْسِدُونَ فِى ٱلْأَرْضِ ۚ أُو۟لَٰٓئِكَ هُمُ ٱلْخَٰسِرُونَ (٢٧) كَيْفَ تَكْفُرُونَ بِٱللَّهِ وَكُنتُمْ أَمْوَٰتًا فَأَحْيَٰكُمْ ۖ ثُمَّ يُمِيتُكُمْ ثُمَّ يُحْيِيكُمْ ثُمَّ إِلَيْهِ تُرْجَعُونَ (٢٨) هُوَ ٱلَّذِى خَلَقَ لَكُم مَّا فِى ٱلْأَرْضِ جَمِيعًا ثُمَّ ٱسْتَوَىٰٓ إِلَى ٱلسَّمَآءِ فَسَوَّىٰهُنَّ سَبْعَ سَمَٰوَٰتٍ ۚ وَهُوَ بِكُلِّ شَىْءٍ عَلِيمٌ (٢٩

"Those who break God's Covenant after it is ratified, and who sunder what God has ordered to be joined, and do mischief on earth: These cause loss (only) to themselves. How can you reject the faith in God? See that you were without life; then will He cause you to die, and will again bring you to life; and again to Him will you return. It is He Who hath created for you all things that are on earth; moreover His design comprehended the heavens, for He gave order and perfection to the seven firmaments; and of all things He hath perfect knowledge". (Qur'an 2:27-29).

Mankind should be grateful and praise his Creator.

وَٱلْحَمْدُ لِلَّهِ رَبِّ ٱلْعَٰلَمِينَ

"And Praise to God, the Lord and Cherisher of the Worlds". (Qur'an 37:182).

Avoid hypocrisy and be truthful. The Qur'an says,

1.   وَلَا تَلْبِسُواْ ٱلْحَقَّ بِٱلْبَٰطِلِ وَتَكْتُمُواْ ٱلْحَقَّ وَأَنتُمْ تَعْلَمُونَ

"And cover not Truth with falsehood, nor conceal the Truth when ye know (what it is)". (Qur'an 2:42).

Trust in Allah.

قُل لَّن يُصِيبَنَآ إِلَّا مَا كَتَبَ ٱللَّهُ لَنَا هُوَ مَوْلَىٰنَا وَعَلَى ٱللَّهِ فَلْيَتَوَكَّلِ ٱلْمُؤْمِنُونَ

"Say: "Nothing will happen to us except what God has decreed for us: He is our Protector": and on God let the Believers put their trust". (Qur'an 9:51).

Establish prayer and pay charity –due.

وَأَقِيمُواْ ٱلصَّلَوٰةَ وَءَاتُواْ ٱلزَّكَوٰةَ وَٱرْكَعُواْ مَعَ ٱلرَّٰكِعِينَ

"And be steadfast in prayer; practice regular charity; and bow down to your heads with those who bow down (in worship). (Qur'an 2:43).

One of the major principles of theo-ethics or relation to the Creator is to not have doubt in His existence or power. The Qur'an says,

ٱلْحَقُّ مِن رَّبِّكَ فَلَا تَكُن مِّنَ ٱلْمُمْتَرِينَ

"The Truth comes from God alone so be not of those who doubt" (Qur'an 3:60).

SOCIO-ETHICS:

Socio-ethics is the relationship of a person with society. We are all social entities. This means, we are members of a society. Our relationships are based upon dignity, integrity, moral values, cooperation, support, and environmental protection. The stronger we are in our socio-ethics, the closer we get to Allah, the Creator. This is done by serving and being an active member of society. According to the late Dr. Shari Ati, the prominent sociologist of the twentieth century, the Qur'an begins with the name of Allah, as we read in the name of Allah, *Most gracious most Mericful*. The Qur'an ends with the aaya (verse) *Al'Nas* (people). As we read at the end of the Qur'an:

مِنَ ٱلْجِنَّةِ وَٱلنَّاسِ

"Among Jinns, and among People". (Qur'an 114:6).

This supports the idea that Allah is the God of the people. The Qur'an is not just for men of knowledge, a specific group, or religious people, it is for mankind. The Qur'an mentions in the same last chapter, saying,

قُلْ أَعُوذُ بِرَبِّ ٱلنَّاسِ (١) مَلِكِ النَّاسِ (٢) إِلَـهِ ٱلنَّاسِ (٣)

"Say: I seek refuge with the Lord and cherisher of mankind, The King or Ruler of mankind, The God or Judge of mankind". (Qur'an 114:1-3).

Understanding this concept makes us more responsible for the well-being of others, because we or "I" are people. If others are happy and prosperous, "I" will be prosperous. It is important to note that there is a relationship between theo-ethics and socio-ethics. That means whatever we do to people, we have to be God-conscious. We have to see Him present in our mind, in order to be good and fulfill justice. If we take Him out of our mind, we will go astray and look only at our own self-interest, as it is very natural for humanity. Psychologically, Islam is the religion of people regardless of their gender, race, ethnicity, economic status, or language. In this relation, one has to be a firm believer in Allah and his Messenger in order to cement his approach to others with dignity and integrity. The following are important to socio-ethics.

Avoid social hypocrisy: That is lying, betraying trust, breaking promises, and safeguarding the tongue to not utter vulgar language. The Qur'an says, "And cover not truth with falsehood, nor conceal the truth when you know what it is" (Qur'an 2:42). You are trying to be a trustworthy person in relation to other people and secure their trust to safeguard one personality.

إِنَّ ٱللَّهَ يَأْمُرُكُمْ أَن تُؤَدُّواْ ٱلْأَمَـٰنَـٰتِ إِلَىٰٓ أَهْلِهَا

"God commands you to render back your trusts to those to whom they're due" (Qur'an 4:58).

Promises define another social concept that distinguishes a positive from a negative personality. The Qur'an says,

يَـٰٓأَيُّهَا ٱلَّذِينَ ءَامَنُوٓاْ أَوْفُواْ بِٱلْعُقُودِ

"O you who believer fulfill all your promises/
obligations" (Qur'an 5:1).

Another aspect of hypocrisy is vulgar language that psychologically damages one's personality in public. The Qur'an says,

لاَّ يُحِبُّ ٱللَّهُ ٱلْجَهْرَ بِٱلسُّوٓءِ مِنَ ٱلْقَوْلِ إِلاَّ مَن ظُلِمَ وَكَانَ ٱللَّهُ سَمِيعًا عَلِيمًا (١٤٨)

"God loves not that evil should be noised abroad in public speech except where injustice has been done, for God is He who hears and knows all things" (Qur'an 4:148).

Also, the Qur'an dictates that by following the role model of the Prophet and absorbing his personality characteristics, people would be in a good mood and would approach other people with gentle gestures. The Qur'an says,

وَإِنَّكَ لَعَلَىٰ خُلُقٍ عَظِيمٍ

"And though (standest) on an exalted standard
of character" (Qur'an 68:4).

Social hygiene: This is not only vital for our health, but also for social interactions that make people psychological likable. As the Qur'an says,

إِنَّ ٱللَّهَ يُحِبُّ ٱلتَّوَّابِينَ وَيُحِبُّ ٱلْمُتَطَهِّرِينَ (٢٢٢)

"God loves those who turn to Him constantly and He loves those who keep themselves pure and clean" (Qur'an 2:222).

Time management: This is another aspect of social interactions that make an individual steadfast, constant, and professional at all times. The Qur'an says,

وَٱلْعَصْرِ (١) إِنَّ ٱلْإِنسَٰنَ لَفِى خُسْرٍ (٢)

"By the token of time, verily man is in loss" (Qur'an 103:1-2).

This means that when we avoid wasting time, there is a socio-psychological principle that needs to be valued highly for achieving our goal without hesitation. Time never comes back and we are getting closer and closer to death. Ironically, we do not know the time, date, hour, or place of our final departure from this world. Psychologically, one always has to be in a state of alert, being efficient, not lazy. The Prophet prayed to not be lazy, incapable, fearful, jealous and problems of old age.

Behaving justly and fulfill justice among others: The Qur'an says,

وَإِذَا حَكَمْتُم بَيْنَ ٱلنَّاسِ أَن تَحْكُمُواْ بِٱلْعَدْلِ

"When you judge between people that you judge with justice" (Qur'an 4:58).

Staying away from racial and gender prejudices: Allah condemns this behavior and people are all creations of Allah and He knows and acknowledges them based on the basis of piety. He says in the Qur'an,

يَـٰٓأَيُّهَا ٱلنَّاسُ إِنَّا خَلَقْنَـٰكُم مِّن ذَكَرٍ وَأُنثَىٰ وَجَعَلْنَـٰكُمْ شُعُوبًا وَقَبَآئِلَ لِتَعَارَفُوٓا۟
إِنَّ أَكْرَمَكُمْ عِندَ ٱللَّهِ أَتْقَىٰكُمْ إِنَّ ٱللَّهَ عَلِيمٌ خَبِيرٌ

"O mankind! We created you from a single (pair) of a male and female, and made you into nations and tribes, that you may know each other (not that you may despise each other). Verily the most honored of you in the sight of God is (he who is) the most righteous of you. And God has full knowledge and is well acquainted (with all things)" (Qur'an 49:13).

Suspicion: This is another principle of socio-ethics because suspicion can lead to bad things. Suspicion can lead to false judgment, animosity, and a bad heart. Allah forbids people to have suspicions, to spy, and to gossip. The Qur'an says,

يَـٰٓأَيُّهَا ٱلَّذِينَ ءَامَنُوا۟ ٱجْتَنِبُوا۟ كَثِيرًا مِّنَ ٱلظَّنِّ إِنَّ بَعْضَ ٱلظَّنِّ إِثْمٌ وَلَا
تَجَسَّسُوا۟ وَلَا يَغْتَب بَّعْضُكُم بَعْضًا أَيُحِبُّ أَحَدُكُمْ أَن يَأْكُلَ لَحْمَ أَخِيهِ
مَيْتًا فَكَرِهْتُمُوهُ وَٱتَّقُوا۟ ٱللَّهَ إِنَّ ٱللَّهَ تَوَّابٌ رَّحِيمٌ (١٢)

"O you who believe! Avoid suspicion as much (as possible): for suspicion in some cases is a sign of sin: and spy not on each other, nor speak ill of each other behind their backs. Would any of you like to eat the flesh of his dead brother? Nay, ye would abhor it...But fear God: for God is Oft-Returning, most Merciful" (Qur'an 49:12).

PSYCHO-ETHICS

Psycho-ethics is the relationship of mankind to himself. It's important to know for the study of psycho-ethics that God says,

وَلَقَدْ خَلَقْنَا ٱلْإِنسَـٰنَ وَنَعْلَمُ مَا تُوَسْوِسُ بِهِ نَفْسُهُ وَنَحْنُ أَقْرَبُ إِلَيْهِ مِنْ حَبْلِ ٱلْوَرِيدِ (١٦

"And indeed We have created man, and We know whatever thoughts his inner self develops, and We are closer to him than (his) jugular vein." (Qur'an 50:16).

At the same time, He is not only closer to our jugular vein but He is also the protector of mankind. God says in the Qur'an,

$$\text{إِنَّ اللَّهَ لَهُ مُلْكُ السَّمَـٰوَاتِ وَالْأَرْضِ يُحْيِ وَيُمِيتُ وَمَا لَكُم مِّن دُونِ اللَّهِ مِن وَلِيٍّ وَلَا نَصِيرٍ (١١٦)}$$

"Indeed, to Allah belongs the dominion of the heavens and the earth. He gives life and causes death. And you have not besides Allah any protector or any helper". (Qur'an 9:116).

He is the one who gives life and causes death, and then gives life again. No one else has that power over mankind but Him. The Qur'an says,

$$\text{كَيْفَ تَكْفُرُونَ بِاللَّهِ وَكُنتُمْ أَمْوَاتًا فَأَحْيَاكُمْ ثُمَّ يُمِيتُكُمْ ثُمَّ يُحْيِيكُمْ ثُمَّ إِلَيْهِ تُرْجَعُونَ (٢٨)}$$

"How can you disbelieve in Allah when you were lifeless and He brought you to life; then He will cause you to die, then He will bring you (back) to life, and then to Him you will be returned." (Qur'an 2:28).

Allah is most Gracious and most Merciful. The only sin that he will not forgive is when mankind associates anything with Him. He created the heaven and the earth, He granted laws to all his creation, He has the power to forgive, but not to those who commit polytheism,

$$\text{إِنَّ اللَّهَ لَا يَغْفِرُ أَن يُشْرَكَ بِهِ وَيَغْفِرُ مَا دُونَ ذَٰلِكَ لِمَن يَشَاءُ وَمَن يُشْرِكْ بِاللَّهِ فَقَدِ افْتَرَىٰ إِثْمًا عَظِيمًا}$$

"Indeed, Allah does not forgive association with Him, but He forgives what is less than that for whom He wills. And he who associates others with Allah has certainty fabricated a tremendous sin." (Qur'an 4:48).

He forgives and amend when people realize their mistakes or sins, and He eradicates all sins when people repent. He says,

وَهُوَ ٱلَّذِى يَقْبَلُ ٱلتَّوْبَةَ عَنْ عِبَادِهِ وَيَعْفُواْ عَنِ ٱلسَّيِّئَاتِ وَيَعْلَمُ مَا تَفْعَلُونَ (٢٥

"And it is He who accepts repentance from his servants and pardons misdeeds, and He knows what you do." (Qur'an 42:25).

Allah is Eternal. He is always alive, and He never goes to sleep or gets tired. He constantly watches His creation.

ٱللَّهُ لَا إِلَـٰهَ إِلَّا هُوَ ٱلْحَىُّ ٱلْقَيُّومُ
لَا تَأْخُذُهُ سِنَةٌ وَلَا نَوْمٌ
لَّهُ مَا فِى ٱلسَّمَـٰوَٰتِ وَمَا فِى ٱلْأَرْضِ
مَن ذَا ٱلَّذِى يَشْفَعُ عِندَهُ
إِلَّا بِإِذْنِهِ يَعْلَمُ مَا بَيْنَ أَيْدِيهِمْ وَمَا خَلْفَهُمْ
وَلَا يُحِيطُونَ بِشَىْءٍ مِّنْ عِلْمِهِ إِلَّا بِمَا شَآءَ
وَسِعَ كُرْسِيُّهُ ٱلسَّمَـٰوَٰتِ وَٱلْأَرْضَ
وَلَا يَـُٔودُهُ حِفْظُهُمَا وَهُوَ ٱلْعَلِىُّ ٱلْعَظِيمُ

"Allah-there is no deity except Him, the Ever-Living, the Sustainer of (all) existence. Neither drowsiness overtakes Him nor sleeps. To Him belongs whatever is in the heavens and whatever is on the earth. Who is it that can intercede with Him except by His permission? He knows what is (presently) before them and what will be after them, and they encompass not a thing of His knowledge except for what He wills. His Kursi, Throne or Seat of Knowledge) extends over the heavens and the earth, and their preservation tires Him not. And He is the Most High, the Most Great." (Qur'an 2:255).

Every living thing is dying but Allah is Eternal; death is a sign of realization of faith. The Qur'an says,

كُلُّ مَنْ عَلَيْهَا فَانٍ (٢٦) وَيَبْقَىٰ وَجْهُ رَبِّكَ ذُو ٱلْجَلَـٰلِ وَٱلْإِكْرَامِ (٢٧

"Everyone upon the earth will perish and there will remain the Face of your Lord, Owner of Majesty and Honor" (Qur'an 55:26-27).

Everything that has been created is praising the Creator, but mankind does not see that.

$$\text{تُسَبِّحُ لَهُ ٱلسَّمَٰوَٰتُ ٱلسَّبْعُ وَٱلْأَرْضُ وَمَن فِيهِنَّ}$$
$$\text{وَإِن مِّن شَىْءٍ إِلَّا يُسَبِّحُ بِحَمْدِهِ وَلَٰكِن لَّا تَفْقَهُونَ تَسْبِيحَهُمْ}$$
$$\text{إِنَّهُ كَانَ حَلِيمًا غَفُورًا}$$

"The seven heavens and the earth and whatever is in them exalt Him. And there is not a thing except that it exalts (Allah) by His praise, but you do not understand their (way of) exalting. Indeed, He is ever Forbearing and Forgiving." (Qur'an 17:44).

Allah is praised by all His angels and they are constantly praising and bowing down to Him.

$$\text{وَتَرَى ٱلْمَلَٰئِكَةَ حَآفِّينَ مِنْ حَوْلِ ٱلْعَرْشِ يُسَبِّحُونَ بِحَمْدِ رَبِّهِمْ وَقُضِىَ}$$
$$\text{بَيْنَهُم بِٱلْحَقِّ وَقِيلَ ٱلْحَمْدُ لِلَّهِ رَبِّ ٱلْعَٰلَمِينَ}$$

"And you will see the angels surrounding the Throne, exalting (Allah) with praise of their Lord. And it will be judged between them in truth, and it will be said, "(All) praise to Allah, Lord of the worlds." (Qur'an 39:75).

Allah never gets tired of recreation of His creation, or we call it in Islamic philosophy, occasionalism. The Qur'an says,

$$\text{أَفَعَيِينَا بِٱلْخَلْقِ ٱلْأَوَّلِ بَلْ هُمْ فِى لَبْسٍ مِّنْ خَلْقٍ جَدِيدٍ}$$

"Did We fail in the first creation? But they are in confusion over a new creation". (Qur'an 50:15).

Allah is the source of knowledge. He created the heaven and the earth, and what is in- between them. Therefore, human knowledge cannot be compared to the power of His wisdom and universal knowledge:

يَعْلَمُ مَا بَيْنَ أَيْدِيهِمْ وَمَا خَلْفَهُمْ وَلَا يُحِيطُونَ بِهِ عِلْمًا

"Allah knows what is (presently) before them and what will be after them, but they do not encompass it in knowledge." (Qur'an 20:110).

Whoever does a good job that is for his own benefit and if someone does a bad job, that is for his own loss. God never oppresses His creation:

مَّنْ عَمِلَ صَـٰلِحًا فَلِنَفْسِهِ وَمَنْ أَسَآءَ فَعَلَيْهَا وَمَا رَبُّكَ بِظَلَّٰمٍ لِّلْعَبِيدِ

"Whoever does righteousness-it is for his (own) soul; and whoever does not (does so) against it. And your Lord is not ever unjust to (His) servants." (Qur'an 41:46).

Mankind should realize the fact that Allah knows whatever we say openly or whatever we hide, and this what the true study of mind and psychology is. The Qur'an says,

إِنَّهُ يَعْلَمُ ٱلْجَهْرَ مِنَ ٱلْقَوْلِ وَيَعْلَمُ مَا تَكْتُمُونَ

"Indeed, He knows what is declared of speech, and He knows what you conceal." (Qur'an 21:110).

In His final revelation, He sends his message to humanity very clearly to bond with Him with honesty and integrity. The Book was sent to people to truly worship Him, not associate anything with Him, and guide themselves for felicity and happiness, in this life and secure Hereafter. The Qur'an says,

إِنَّ فِى هَٰذَا لَبَلَٰغًا لِّقَوْمٍ عَٰبِدِينَ

"Indeed, in this (Qur'an) is notification for people who worship." (Qur'an 21:106).

DREAMING

According to Islam, dreaming is a miracle from God in human beings. Dreaming is a science that deals with human mind while asleep that can be learned through not only knowledge but through wisdom. This wisdom is also given from God to mankind as he did to Prophet Joseph. The Qur'an says,

وَكَذَٰلِكَ مَكَّنَّا لِيُوسُفَ فِى ٱلْأَرْضِ وَلِنُعَلِّمَهُ مِن تَأْوِيلِ ٱلْأَحَادِيثِ وَٱللَّهُ غَالِبٌ عَلَىٰ أَمْرِهِ وَلَٰكِنَّ أَكْثَرَ ٱلنَّاسِ لَا يَعْلَمُونَ

"Thus did We establish Joseph in the land, that We might teach him the interpretation of stories (dreams)" (Qur'an 12:21).

According to Islam, dreaming is a sign of Prophethood; God signaled the Prophet in his dream and gave him the good news of being the last Prophet. The Qur'an says,

مَّا كَانَ مُحَمَّدٌ أَبَآ أَحَدٍ مِّن رِّجَالِكُمْ وَلَٰكِن رَّسُولَ ٱللَّهِ وَخَاتَمَ ٱلنَّبِيِّـۧنَ وَكَانَ ٱللَّهُ بِكُلِّ شَىْءٍ عَلِيمًا

"Muhammad is not the father of any of your men, but (he is) the Apostle of God, and the Seal of the Prophets: and God has full knowledge of all things" (Qur'an 33:40).

When the Prophet once woke up, he narrated this dream to his wife Khadjah and she told him that he would be awaiting good news.

According to Islam, there are natural and unnatural dreams. Natural dreams take place due to the energy received during the day, the meals eaten, illnesses, and other nutrition delicacies. In this type of dream, the brain rests like any other physical part of the body. Unnatural dreams are caused by mixture of four matters: blood, black bile, phlegm, and anxiety.

Too much consumption of heavy food, little sleep or even long hours of sleep may cause unnatural dreams. According to Islamic scholars, dreams will make a person aware of the truth of the matter and the end of an affair can be exploited. They divided this into four categories:

1. Commanding dreams tells a person to do or perform an action.
2. Avoiding dreams that warns the person to avoid certain tasks.
3. Warnings of fear and danger.
4. Conveyance of good news.

The Prophet of Islam mentioned that there are three kinds of dreams: One that God Almighty gives good news to the believers in their lifetime. Second, is Satanic temptation that makes people sad, and third, are scattered and distressed dreams. It has been recommended that in order to have natural and positive dreams, one should maintain a balanced diet and perform his/her night prayers. It is also recommended by the Prophet of Islam to not expose unnatural dreams to others; instead keep it to yourself and pray this:

"I seek refuge from Satan the cursed one"

In these types of dreams, the meaning is not solid or interpretative. It is only through natural dreams that people are informed of some news with varying duration after their dreams. There are blessed dreams that, depending on the spiritual level of the individual, the person will dream of good things and dream good results, and there are bad dreams that are contrary to this.

CONCLUSION

Psychology is the study of mind and this is exactly what the Qur'an put a great emphasis between the relationship of man and his Creator and the role faith plays intellectually and spiritually in our lives.

The Qur'an is a book of wisdom and it includes all aspects of human life. Religion, as a matter of fact is an intellectual property that cannot be seen. So the mind cannot be seen. Human being is a curious creature. This curiosity elaborated in the story of Abraham that he wanted to find the Truth for himself. Finding the truth is a principle of science and research. Islamic psychology is based on three principles, namely, theo-ethics, socio-ethics, and psyco-ethics, which discuss human relations from a psychological point of you. It is the mind that relates to all aspects of life. Therefore, Islamic psychology deals with all spheres that originate from God alone. For that, ego or self plays a major role and makes mankind responsible for all his actions. Since Islam is a religion of unity then all processes of mind inter-relate to not only self, but also to God and society. Therefore, like any other field of knowledge, it is hard to separate psychology or the study of mind from other life principles. As a matter of fact it is the mind that regulates other affairs, being good or bad. Islamic psychology emphases on making humans responsible for their inner soul activities, which that lead either to felicity or destruction. Since religion is an intellectual property then the study of mind is also a spiritual and intellectually property.

REFERENCES

Understanding the Psychological Concept In Islam

1. *Science Proves the Healing Power of Prayer.* (2015, March 31). Retrieved July 27, 2-16, from Newsmax Health: www.newsmax.com/Health/Headline/prayer-health-faith-medicine/2015/03/31/id/635623
2. Schiffman, R. (2012, March 19th). *Why People Who Pray Are Healthier Than Those Who Don't.* Retrieved September 16th, 2016, from Huffington Post: www.huffingtonpost.com/richard-schiffman/why-people-who-pray-are-healthier-b_1197313.html

The Nature of God in Islam

3. (n.d). Retrieved October 27th, 2016, from Does it Mean God? : www.godallah.com
4. Al-Fârûqī I.R. (1982). Al Tawhid: Its Implications for Thought and Life. The International Institute of Islamic Thought. P. 2-3.
5. Armstrong, K. (1993). A History of God, New York: Ballantine Books. P. 143

Tawhid: Oneness of God

6. Ati, S. (1979). *On the Sociology of Islam.* (H. Algar, Trans.) Oneonta, New York: Mizan Press.

7. Bakhtiar, L. (1993). *God's Will Be Done*. (Vol. 3). Chicago, IL. The Institute of Traditional Psychoethics and Guidance.
8. Al-Fârûqī I.R. (1982). *Al Tawhid: Its Implications for Thought and Life*. The International Institute of Islamic Thought.
9. Bakhtiar, L. (1993). *God' Will Be Done*. (Vol. 3). Chicago, IL. The Institute of Traditional Psychoethics and Guidance

Nature vs. Nurture

10. (n.d.). *Change in Mother's Mental State can Influence Her Baby's Development Before and After Birth*. Retrieved November 1st, 2016, from Association for Psychological Science: http://www.psychologicalscience.org/news/releases/a-fetus-can-sense-moms-psychological-state.html#.WHkscym-pUQ

Patience is a Virtue

11. Barry, C. (n.d.). *The Top 60 Buddha Quotes.* Retrieved October 27, 2016, from Addicted2Success: www.addicted2success.com/quotes/the-top-60-buddha-quotes

Grief

12. Meek, Will. (2012, October 18th). *Real Stages of Grief.* Retrieved November 3rd, 2016 from Psychology Today. https://www.psychologytoday.com/blog/notes-self/201210/real-stages-grief

Sufism

13. Culliford, Larry. (2015, June 1st). *What is Sufism? https://www.psychologytoday.com/blog/spiritual-wisdom-secular-times/201506/what-is-sufism*

14. Culliford, Larry. (2015, June 1st). *What is Sufism? https://www. psychologytoday.com/blog/spiritual-wisdom-secular-times/201506/ what-is-sufism*

Personality Development

15. Hart, Michael. (1978). *The 100, A Ranking of the Most Influential Persons in History.* New York, NY. Kensington Publisher. Pg. 3
16. Ansari, Muhammad. (1973). *The Quranic Foundations and Structure of Muslim Society.* (Vol 1). Pakistan. Trade and Industry Publications.
17. Mayo Clinic Staff. (n.d.) *Narcissistic Personality Disorder.* Retrieved November 20th, 2016 from Mayo Clinic. http://www.mayoclinic. org/diseases-conditions/narcissistic-personality-disorder/basics/ definition/con-20025568

Male and Female Brain

18. Prigg, M. (2015, November 30). *Men are from Mars....and so are women! Scans reveal there is NO overall difference between the brains of the sexes.* Retrieved October 28, 2016, from Daily Mail: www.dailymail.co.uk/sciencetech/article-3340123/ Male-vs-female-brain-Not-valid-distinction-study-says/html
19. Wheeling, K. (2015, November 30). *The brains of men and women aren't really that different, study finds.* Retrieved October 15th, 2016, from Science Magazine: www.sciencemag.org/news/2015/11/ brains-men-and-women-aren-t-really-different-study-finds

Health and Stress Management

20. Dockrill, P. (2016, May 6). *Eating Less Improves Mood, Sleep, and Sex Drive in Healthy People, Study Finds.* Retrieved September 17,2016, from Science Alert: www.sciencealert.com/eating-less- improves-mood-sleep-and-sex-drive-in-healthy-people-studyfinds

21. *Fasting and Health: Ramadan Fasting-Key to Good Health.* (n.d.). Retrieved from ww.Islamicoccasion.com

Human Sexuality

22. *Family Structure in Islam*, (2012, July). Retrieved from http:// islamicencyclopedia.org/public/islamic-discussions/index.php?p=/ discussion/279
23. Maududi, Sayyid. (2009). *The Rights and Duties of Spouses.* (Third Edition). Markazi Maktaba Islami Publishers.
24. Afza, Nazhat.(1993). *The Position of Woman in Islam.* (Third Edition). Islamic Book Publishers.
25. Bucaille, M. (1979). *The Bible, the Qur'an, and Science.* Islamic Book Service

Homo Sexuality

26. Park,Alice.(2012,20th July).*HIV Continues to Spread Among Gay Men, Studies Show.* Retrieved from http://healthland.time.com/2012/07/20/ hiv-continues-to-spread-among-gay-men-studies-show/

Cognition

27. Bucaille, M. (1979). *The Bible, the Qur'an, and Science.* Islamic Book Service.
28. *Child Development and Early Learning,* Fourth Edition. (n.d.). Retrieved September 22,2016, from Facts for Life: www. factsforlifeglobal.org/03/
29. Cognitive Development. (n.d.). Retrieved from http://www. healthofchildren.com/C/Cognitive-Development.html
30. Al-Fârûqī I.R. (1982). Al Tawhid: Its Implications for Thought and Life. The International Institute of Islamic Thought.

Humanism

31. Boisard, M. (1988). *Humanism in Islam.* United States. American Trust Publications

Psychodynamics

32. Coon, D. (1997). *Essentials of Psychology.* (Vol. 7). Pacific Grove, CA: Brooks/Cole Publishing Company
33. Bakhtiar, L. (1993). *God' Will Be Done.* (Vol. 3). Chicago, IL. The Institute of Traditional Psychoethics and Guidance

Nafs

34. Ali, Muhammad. (1973). *The Holy Qur'an.* (6th Edition). Lahor, Pakistan. Ahmadiyyah Anjuman Ish'at Islam Lahore Inc. US.
35. Sherali, H.D. (2014). *Spiritual Discourses.* Bloomington, IN: AuthorHouse

Printed in the United States
By Bookmasters